STAY

FREE

Why Society Can't Survive Without God

(Gal 5:1)

Mark Fairley

1

"So Christ has truly set us free. Now make sure that you stay free, and don't get tied up again in slavery to the law." - Gal 5:1

CONTENTS

INTRODUCTION

The statistics are devastating.

Depression now affects 121 million people worldwide.

World suicide rates have risen by 60% in the last 45 years. Failed suicide attempts are 20 times as frequent and suicide is now the third leading cause of death in young adults.

Alcohol abuse has risen to the point that almost a tenth of all deaths worldwide in the 15-29 age group can be attributed to it.

Levels of national debt are soaring. Globally, public debt as a percentage of GDP in OECD countries went from hovering around 70% in the 1990s to around 110% today. Even previously stable economies now have massive budget deficits and are threatening to collapse.

The cost of policing has risen by 40% in the last decade.

Benefits paid out by the government have risen 25% in the last decade.

In Western countries illegitimate birth rates are rising towards the 50% mark and marriages increasingly fail, if entered into at all.

(All statistics provided by the World Health Organisation, House of Commons Research Papers & Global Finance Magazine)

What is going wrong with the world? Why is society crumbling? When I interviewed members of the public prior to the launch of this book about whether they thought the world was becoming a better or worse place to live, the vast majority said "worse". Almost without fail, *everyone* believed that society has degenerated somehow within their lifetime. The world used to seem friendlier, less stressful, more honest, less fraught with dangers, kindlier and perhaps most tellingly, somehow more innocent.

When I asked these same people to identify where things went wrong however, they all had very different answers. Some blamed parents for not raising their kids properly. Others blamed the kids themselves for being lazy and not having enough respect. Others blamed ambitious and corrupt politicians. Others greedy bankers. Others teachers for not doing their job properly. Others religion for being the cause of all the violence the world. Some talked vaguely about a lack of community. Some even blamed climate change. In other words, although everyone agreed that the world is breaking apart, no one really knew agreed on what the problem was. And not understanding the problem, there could be no agreement on a solution.

I believe there is a beautiful, elegant and simple answer. And perhaps I can explain it like this:

Imagine a kitchen tap (faucet) is left running in a house and the water starts to flood the building. You can attempt to solve the flooding by building barricades, putting up sandbags, isolating rooms, setting up pumps and drainage facilities, asking the neighbours to come with buckets on a 24 hour rota system and you can spend endless time and energy dealing with the consequences of the problem...OR...you can just turn off the tap.

There's a root to all this disintegration in the world and this book aims to show exactly why changing one thing will change everything.

SECTION 1
KNOWING THE TRUTH

CHAPTER 1
OUR CORRUPTED HEARTS

This is a rock.

There's nothing special about it; it's just an average rock. It doesn't really do much. It just sits there. Like a rock. So if I were to come to you and say, " *this rock is a really evil rock! Don't turn your back on it for a second or it'll come and get you!"* you would either think I was joking or absolutely crazy. And you would of course be right because obviously there's no such thing as an evil rock. And the reason rocks can't be evil is that they have no awareness of what we call the MORAL LAW – they have no sense of right and wrong. And even if they did, they have no mind or free-will of their own to do anything other than sit there like a rock. And it's for these reasons that we can say that this rock is *morally neutral.*

All the basic stuff that the world is made of is morally neutral. Wood, grass, cotton, metal, stone, vegetables, plants, earth, clouds, you name it. And pretty much everything we make out of that stuff is also morally neutral - trains, musical instruments, shoes, hats, dinners, computers, footballs, plastic chairs, wooden chairs, barbecues, television sets, windows, airplanes, stuffed animals, toothpaste and light bulbs.

It's true we sometimes call these things 'good' or 'bad', but we don't mean that in a moral sense. We can say a hat is a bad hat but all we mean is that it doesn't suit our purpose or we don't think it's fashionable or it isn't made very well. When we say a hat is a bad hat what we *don't* mean is that we suspect it could lie or steal or murder us at any given moment.

For something to be considered good or evil in a moral sense it must have two things:

1) It must have a conscious awareness of what right and wrong actually is – in other words it must *know* the MORAL LAW.
2) It must have the *free-will* to break that MORAL LAW.

We innately know this is true. Say someone throws a rock at you and hits you on the back of the head. Would you blame the rock for the injury or would you blame the person who threw it? Of course, you blame the person who threw it. Why? Because they were the ones who:

1) knew about the MORAL LAW and who... (knowledge)
2) chose to break it.   (free-will)

Therefore, the person is the moral agent. The rock didn't know it was being thrown, it didn't know whether that was a good or bad thing, it had no part in the decision to be thrown, no strength to resist being thrown and no freedom to do anything other than be thrown. Therefore it has no moral responsibility.

We can represent the whole thing using this diagram.

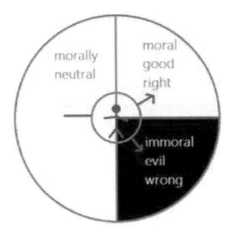

As the moral agent, the human being has the ability to take the morally neutral things that would fill up the left hand side of the diagram like rocks and vegetables and chairs and bottles and manipulate them for good or evil. The human being both *knows* about good and evil and has the *free-will* to *choose* between those options.

All neutral objects can be used for good or evil by moral agents in this way. For example, clothes are made from morally neutral fabric. There's nothing good or evil about a bit of cotton or polyester. But that fabric can be turned into warm blankets for homeless people, which is good, or it can be designed or worn in such a way to incite lust, which is bad. Jumbo jets are morally neutral and can be used to ferry organ donations to hospitals, which is good, or they can be flown into buildings causing death and destruction, which is bad. Morally neutral musical instruments can be used to worship God, which is good, or Satan, which is bad. Even things that people would typically associate with evil actions, like guns and knives, are morally neutral. We can use knives to cut up food to feed a child or free a dolphin tangled in fishing nets, which is good, or to stab people, which is bad. And as the phrase goes, *"guns don't kill people; people kill people."*

The moral responsibility is always with the human being creating or using the items; the one who is capable of choosing between the moral options - not the items themselves. Think of neutral items as being morally malleable, adaptable, flexible or soft. They can be shaped by us in any way we want and used for any purpose we want.

THE HUMAN HEART

Whether a human being acts morally or immorally with those objects is rooted in, what might be called, the human heart.

You see, we are all made up of three parts - body, soul and spirit. The body is your blood, tissue and bone. It is basically a perishable container for the real *you*. The real you is what's inside and it's made up of your soul and spirit.

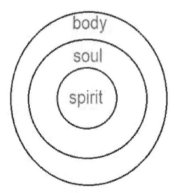

The **soul** is your mind, your will and emotions. It's the part of you that makes decisions. It's the part that ***chooses***.

The **spirit** is the part that contains your conscience and what some might call your intuition. It's the part that instinctively *knows* the moral law. It is your real centre and it's the part of you that is capable of communing with God.

The Bible refers to the soul and spirit collectively as 'the heart' of a person. So within every human heart is the ability to *know* good and evil and to *choose* between good and evil.

A healthy human heart works like this: At the core there is a healthy spirit with a healthy conscience (strong knowledge of right and wrong) and a connection with God. That spirit then controls the soul (mind & will) throughout the decision making process and then, having made a good moral decision in their heart, that in turn controls how they act externally with their body. Like dropping a stone into a pond, there's a ripple effect that starts at the core of your being and works its way outwards, ultimately expressing itself in your words and deeds. Your spirit affects your thoughts and decisions which affect your deeds. That's basically the chain reaction. A healthy internal spirit with a strong sense of the moral law leads to good decision making which leads to healthy external behaviour. It's often even said that who a person is on the inside begins to reveal itself on their face.

So you see, the root of all we do, all we are and all we become, starts with what happens in hearts. And if we get that part right, everything else follows. The heart is where the well-spring of your life is. From it flows life or death. Indeed, Proverbs says, *"Guard your heart above all else, for it determines the course of your life" (Proverbs 4:23)*

So taking this principle and working in reverse, if we find people using their body for *immoral* purposes - if we find people lying, cheating, stealing, raping and murdering - what we are witnessing is merely external evidence of inner corruption or impairment in the soul and spirit.

How does the soul and spirit - the heart of a person - become corrupted? I'll give a couple of examples.

CORRUPTED HEARTS

Firstly, our hearts can be corrupted by what we see and hear. By what we absorb. Jesus talked about the eye being a lamp to the soul. Our ears work in a similar way. If we constantly absorb violence, corruption, lies, foul speech, pornography etc. we will become numb to the severity of those things, our conscience will become seared and evil will become normalised. When you are surrounded by darkness, your eyes adjust and you get used to it. You end up living in darkness without really noticing that it's darkness anymore. A similar thing happens with our hearts. When we surround our hearts with evil it becomes normal and we stop realising it's evil.

To counter this threat to our hearts, the Bible implores us to focus and mediate on things that will instead nurture them and bring light. Paul writes, *"And now dear brothers and sisters, one final thing. Fix your thoughts on what is true, and honourable, and right, and pure, and lovely, and admirable. Think about things that are excellent and worth of praise." (Phil 4:8)*

This means we need to use our time to get into the Word of God, to worship, to get recharged in the company of believers and to choose wisely what we are entertained by. What do you choose to listen to? What do you choose to watch? Is it horror? Is it blasphemous? Is it pornographic? Is it distasteful? Be careful. You're corrupting your own heart by filling it with darkness. Make no mistake. You will become like the things that you meditate on, worship, absorb and believe.

Unfortunately, in our world today, it's virtually impossible not to be exposed to corrupting influences whether we go looking for them or not. There's violence all over TV, sexual imagery all over adverts and foul speech everywhere we go. Our culture is becoming increasingly debased by it and the normalisation of evil has undoubtedly affected us negatively to varying extents. But this is all the more reason why we must be intentional in guarding our hearts.

As well as having our hearts corrupted by, what you could call, our environment, it can also be corrupted by our experiences.

Parents get divorced or walk out on children, friends let each other down, boyfriends and girlfriends cheat on each other, someone steals from another, someone lies to another, someone hurts another. All such experiences wound us emotionally and mentally and leave scars. They can often lead us to make bitter vows of retaliation, distrust or contempt.

Having been wounded, people might say, *"I'm never going to trust anyone again"* or *"I'm going to take revenge on that person"* or *"I'm going to always treat the world how it's treated me."* In making these bitter resolutions, our emotional wounds eventually lead to us wounding others. By never giving others our trust. By putting up emotional barriers. By taking out our frustrations and anger on innocent parties. By becoming colder or harder or angrier. Quite simply:

Injured people injure people.

The more sinful a society gets, the more pain people experience, and the more pain they experience, the more they inflict pain on others. So pain becomes contagious. Like a cancer that spreads exponentially throughout society.

When Proverbs says, *"Guard your heart above all else, for it determines the course of your life."* (Prov 4:23) you could add that it will then determine the course of the lives around you too. No man is an island. If you have been wounded at heart it will affect how you treat others.

To counter this threat to our hearts, we need to learn to forgive those who have hurt us, to not make these inner vows of bitterness but to cast all our burdens on Jesus, to learn how to even love those who hate us, to repay evil with good and to pray for those who would do us harm. If we hold onto bitterness, distrust and unforgiveness, we're holding a disease within our hearts that will damage the course of our own lives firstly, and the courses of the lives around us secondly. We will perpetuate the disease.

Jesus said, *"You have heard the law that says, 'Love your neighbour' and hate your enemy. But I say, love your enemies! Pray for those who persecute you! In that way, you will be acting as true children of your Father in heaven. For he gives his sunlight to both the evil and the good, and he sends rain on the just and the unjust alike. If you love only those who love you, what reward is there for that? Even corrupt tax collectors do that much. If you are kind only to your friends, how are you different from anyone else? Even pagans do that. But you are to be perfect, even as your Father in heaven is perfect." (Matt 5:43-48)*

Love for enemies is perhaps the most difficult bit of teaching Jesus ever gave but it's also one of the most important. You can't have a healthy heart until you learn to forgive.

THE SINFUL HEART

So the heart can be corrupted by our environment and our experiences. But the Bible has something even more shocking to tell us about our hearts.

The Bible tells us that our hearts are *born* corrupt!

Not just that they *can* be corrupted, but that they are *naturally* corrupt. The Bible calls it the sinful nature and it tells us that we have inherited it from Adam and Eve - the first humans. Therefore, basically, we *all* start off broken from day one.

This is why you don't need to teach children to lie; the sinful nature is inherent.

You don't need to teach children to take cookies from the cookie jar before dinner; it's inherent.

You don't need to teach them to grab things that another kid is playing with; it's inherent.

You don't need to teach them how to throw a tantrum when they don't get their own way; it's inherent.

Indeed, half the job of a parent is to teach children *not* to lie, *not* to be disobedient, *not* to take things that belong to others and *not* to throw tantrums when they don't get their own way.

Parents need to teach children to *override* their inherent sinful natures. How to be honest even when it won't serve them to be, how to be obedient even when it means self-denial, how to share and give toys to others even when they don't want to. Those are the things that take work. And that's because parents are trying to overcome an *inherent* bent towards selfishness that exists within all human beings.

As the famous proverb says, "to err is human". In Christian parlance that proverb is rendered, "to sin is human." It's natural for us all.

Take a look back at your life and there will be moments that you regret, times when you were wrong and moments when your behaviour fell below the level you would expect of yourself. If a movie were to be made of every deed, word and thought you've ever had, you couldn't bear to watch it - neither could anyone else if it came to their own lives - such would be the shame and guilt that we would all feel at certain points.

What's more, tomorrow you'll sin again. And from this day until the day you die, you'll sin many more times beyond that. No matter how hard you try not to. Because the sinful nature is inherent.

The Bible says*, "For all have sinned; we all fall short of God's glorious standard." (Romans 3:23)*

And the sin begins in our corrupted hearts. Jesus said, *"For from the heart come evil thoughts, murder, adultery, all sexual immorality, theft, lying and slander. These are what defile you." (Matt 15:19-20)*

The heart is where it all begins.

ARE WE WITHOUT HOPE?

You can understand the gravity of what the Bible is saying with this concept of inherent heart corruption.

If we are all broken from the *beginning* and sinfulness is our *natural* disposition, we're pretty much without hope. If it's in our very natures to put self first, how will the world ever be free of greed, lying, theft, adultery and the pain that follows? How can the world ever be at peace if people have it in their very natures to cheat, defraud, gossip and slander? How can the cancer that starts in our own hearts and spreads out into society ever be healed? Try as we might, none of us can fully override our own natures.

This is all very much starting to look hopeless. It looks like we're doomed to continue in the way we always have. With wars and inequality and corruption and all the rest. The story of human history doesn't look like changing any time soon.

The only thing that could really fix this whole problem is if we could somehow be given new hearts. That's where the root of the problem is. We would need a kind of spiritual regeneration. If we had new hearts, a new spirit, we could attain a new nature. And from that new nature we would find ourselves naturally and automatically bent towards generosity, love, honesty and obedience. And that would fix everything.

Imagine it.

Imagine a society where everyone's hearts were naturally intent on selflessness rather than selfishness.

A world where people wouldn't steal from each other but would give to each other. Where people wouldn't incite one another to lust but would put others first. Where the streets would be safe to play in. Where there would be no wars. Where all human hearts would be filled with life, purity, kindliness, honesty, generosity and love.

Fixing the sinful nature would fix everything else about us. New hearts, new natures, regenerated spirits in the hearts of men and women everywhere...that would be like turning off the tap of sin and destruction that automatically flows out from within us. It would heal us and it would heal society.

We would always *know* the right thing and we would always want to *choose* the right thing.

Now here's the best part. The exciting part. The spine-tingling part.

The Bible tells us that all this is possible.

New hearts. Spiritual regeneration. It's not just a nice thought. It can happen!

But it can only happen with God.

We can only really *know* the difference between good and evil with God, and we can only achieve the spiritual regeneration that we need to *choose* good with God.

And that's why ultimately, society can't survive *without* God.

In this first section, we're going to focus on the *knowing* part. We're going to explore how it's only possible to know the difference between good and evil when we acknowledge God.

CHAPTER 2
KNOWING RIGHT & WRONG

Take a look at this apple.

Would you eat this apple? Do you think it would taste good? If you're sensible you wouldn't put this near your mouth because you know just by looking at it, that this is a bad apple. But how do you know that it's bad? Why do you instinctively know that this is rotten and unhealthy?

The reason you know that this is a bad apple is because at some point in your life you've seen a good one, and consequently you know that this one doesn't meet the standard.

If you didn't know what a good apple was meant to look like, you wouldn't know that this one doesn't match the standard. Give this apple to a baby that hasn't seen apples before and the likelihood is that he will take a bite. He doesn't know any better. And if you hadn't seen a good one, you'd be in the same boat. It's only because you have pre-knowledge of a good one that you can recognise all the bad ones. The good becomes a benchmark by which you subconsciously compare the rest.

Indeed, whenever we define *anything* as good or bad, we are instinctively comparing it to an absolute standard like this. A reference point. A benchmark. When we say that something is "good" we're saying it meets the standard and when we say it's "bad" we're saying it falls short of the standard. The absolute good becomes our reference point.

This applies universally. We recognise crooked lines because we've seen straight ones. We measure athletic performances by world records. We measure darkness by how far removed it is from daylight. We always use the absolute good as a benchmark by which we can measure and recognise the bad.

Imagine an alien arrives on earth at midnight and sees this sky.

He might believe that this is as light as it ever gets on planet earth. After all, he would have nothing else to compare it to.

At sunrise however, around 5am, his understanding would change.

Because he now sees the light of the sun, he would now understand that what he previously thought was light wasn't very light at all.

However, by midday, when the sun is highest in the sky, his understanding would change still further:

Only now, having seen absolute light, would he have a *full* understanding of the dark. Only now would he have a *full* appreciation of the difference. What he initially thought was light was actually darkness. He recognises that now. Even what he saw at 5am has turned out to be darkness by comparison.

So a growing understanding of the light has given him a growing understanding of the dark. And only a perfect understanding of light has given a perfect understanding of dark. Once again, the absolute light becomes a reference point or benchmark by which to measure darkness.

THE MORAL BENCHMARK

It's the same with knowing good and evil.

If we're to truly understand good and evil - if we're to have a true sense of morality - we need a benchmark of absolute good as a reference point by which to recognise and measure evil. If we have no knowledge of that benchmark, we can have no real understanding of good or evil at all.

That absolute and perfect benchmark of goodness is God.

God is the *only* objective and absolute reference point of goodness that we know of. Therefore, if we get rid of God as our benchmark, it's not long before we become morally lost. We stop being able to recognise evil.

CS Lewis wrote, *"when a man is getting better he understands more and more clearly the evil that is still left in him. When a man is getting worse, he understands his own badness less and less...this is common sense really. You understand sleep when you are awake, not while you are sleeping...You can understand the nature of drunkenness when you are sober, not when you are drunk. Good people know about both good and evil: bad people do not know about either."* (Mere Christianity)

You have to know God as a reference point of absolute good to truly understand evil and the better you know that Absolute Good, the better you will understand the difference. If that fixed standard of goodness is taken away however, then you actually have no way of knowing what right and wrong or good or evil actually is at all. Those words lose all meaning. So our understanding of what might be called, the MORAL LAW, *completely* depends on our understanding of God.

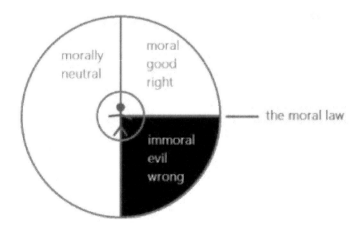

The MORAL LAW stems from God. It's an expression of who He is. He defines what is right and what is wrong. The MORAL LAW is God's law.

American legal philosopher James Wilson put it well when he said, *"it should always be remembered that this [moral] law, natural or revealed, made for men or for nations, flows from the same divine source: it is the law of God."*

Let's put it one final way to fix the point in our minds. You often hear people talking about "moral compasses" - this inner sense of right and wrong that regulates our behaviour. Well, real compasses only work in reference to a fixed point called Magnetic North and the compass gives your bearings in relation to it. If Magnetic North didn't exist as an absolute reference point then the compass would be completely useless and it wouldn't give any direction at all. You would just be left to guess and go your own way.

It's the same with moral compasses - they only work in reference to an objective fixed point of morality called God. Without that absolute fixed reference point of goodness, we have no way of navigating right and wrong or even knowing what those words mean.

Take God away and our diagram changes like this.

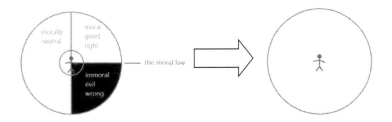

We become lost in an amoral void. Without God, there's no objective MORAL LAW - no objective reference point by which to measure good or evil. Nothing outside of ourselves that we can point to as a benchmark of goodness. No boundaries. No such thing as absolute right and wrong.

All that's left is for each individual to create their own moral code, define their own individual standards of right and wrong, go in whatever direction they think is best, live by their own rules.

In other words, they can just do whatever they want.

Morality becomes whatever you want it to be without God. In other words, it becomes subjective. There are no absolutes under this system; it's all relative. People without God have nothing to refer to except themselves so every person becomes their own standard of goodness; their own moral arbiter. When faced with a moral decision they look inside their hearts and go with whatever feels right to them or whatever they happen to prefer in that moment. So in a sense each person becomes their own god.

And you know what? People quite like that thought.

In fact, our sinful hearts love it. It sounds so liberating! To be free of the restraint of the rigid moral code that God's existence imposes. To be free to create your own. And let's not pretend the MORAL LAW isn't rigid. CS Lewis again wrote, *"there is nothing indulgent about the moral law. It is as hard as nails. It tells you to do the straight thing and it does not seem to care how painful, or dangerous, or difficult it is to do."*

People hate that.

There are times for all of us when we wish morality wasn't so rigid. There are times when we wish it didn't even exist.

When we've done something wrong and need to apologise; when we have a chance to make lots of money dishonestly; when we're consumed with lust for a married woman; when telling a lie would get us off the hook; when we have a chance to download some free stuff instead of paying for it; when there's some tempting chocolate in the refrigerator that doesn't belong to us, when pornography seems so enticing...there are times for all of us when we would love to be free to indulge our sinful natures. Times when we would love to shake off any ideas of a moral law to just do what we wanted. Times when we find ourselves annoyingly having to wrestle with our consciences and trying to blur lines and create grey areas in the MORAL LAW so that we can indeed go ahead and gratify our sinful desires.

Times when we say things to ourselves like, *"They didn't apologise when they wronged me so I don't need to apologise to them and that makes us even." "Musicians are rich, they won't miss a few pennies from my free download." "They're on a diet anyway, I'm doing them a favour eating their chocolate." "If I lie just this once I'll make up for it in other ways later...it's only a white lie anyway." "How much harm does pornography really do?" "And does the MORAL LAW really say...?"* Times when we all try to manipulate, bend or erase the MORAL LAW to accommodate our whims, our situation, and our selfish fancies. Times when, what we'd really like is to be liberated from it altogether so that we can do what we want without guilt or dismay. *"Do what you want".* We can't deny how freeing that sounds.

Do What You Want

But unbeknownst to many people, "do what you want" is actually the golden rule of Satanism. Or in their own words:

"Do what thou wilt shall be the whole of the law."

Remember what Satan told Adam and Eve in Eden? He told them that God with His strict rules about right and wrong was a tyrant and an oppressor and if they broke free from Him and went their own way they could establish their own moral code. They could live how they wanted. They could become their own gods. And he did it by trying to suggest loopholes, blur lines and create grey areas in God's strict instruction. "Did God *really* say you couldn't eat that fruit?"

He tried to paint the abandonment of the MORAL LAW as liberty. Today he does the same thing and it's a message our sinful hearts want to hear.

We want to hear that we can put ourselves first, take that chocolate, download that free music, get our own way, lie to be let off the hook, watch pornography, have sexual encounters with people we've just met, make lots of money with no regard to the lives of others, satisfy our cravings, our lusts, or whims, our fancies and desires. We want to hear that.

This is why it's often said that many people can't find God for the same reason that criminals can't find a police officer. They could really...it's just they don't want to...because they realise that the second they acknowledge a holy God, they instantly become accountable to His objective MORAL LAW. That means that all their self-indulgences and cravings for sin that they currently enjoy would have to come under restraint.

Two Paths

So there are two paths before each of us.

We can accept and submit to God's MORAL LAW and in knowing it better, become ever more enlightened as to the difference between good and evil.

OR

we can reject all notion of Absolute Good to follow our own path instead. We can then formulate our own ideas of morality, make our own rules, do what we want, define our own standards of right and wrong, place ourselves on the thrones of our own lives...become our own gods.

The first path is God's path; the second is Satan's.

Satan's sounds like freedom and that's why so many people take it, but if you take it this will happen:

As you reject any notion of Absolute Good to allow yourself to sin, you'll begin to lose sight of what 'good' and 'evil' actually means. You'll get used to living in darkness and you'll stop recognising that darkness is what you're actually in. You'll find yourself bending or ignoring your self-styled moral code at times to allow yourself to sin when the mood takes you. Your cravings will regularly override it. You will be your own god after all. There will be no one else to answer to. So why not do what makes you happy? Why not 'follow your heart'? You'll do this to the extent that, if you were honest, you'd realise you don't really have a moral code at all and have simply become a slave to your own sinful desires. You'll simply adapt your morality to allow yourself to do whatever you want to do. A fog will descend upon your mind. It will become dark and confused.

You'll find yourself being certain of nothing. You'll insist that you're a good person because you would hate to think of yourself as being anything else. But you'll become like someone who doesn't recognise bad apples because they haven't seen a good one. Or like someone who doesn't recognise a crooked line because they haven't seen a straight one. Or like someone who takes 40 minutes to run a mile long track and thinks they've done rather well because they've never witnessed that others do it in under 4 minutes. In other words, when your only moral benchmark is yourself, you'll stop being able to understand your own sinfulness. You'll lose sight of right and wrong. Your moral compass will break without a reference point. Good and evil will lose their meaning.

Therefore, you'll see no contradiction in calling yourself a good person even when you gossip, slander, cheat, blaspheme, lie or steal or serve yourself. You'll justify your actions always. You'll continue looking at yourself through your own self-constructed, subjective definition of right and wrong, through your own idolatry of self, and will decree confidently that you're a very decent person indeed and that if there's any friction, the fault lies with the other party. As Proverbs says, *"Most men will proclaim every one his own goodness"* (Prov 20:6). Even Adolf Hitler did.

The point is just this: that ultimately, godless people don't just become more evil, but they understand the difference between good and evil less.

They lose sight of *knowledge* the MORAL LAW.

And this is the path that will in the end, lead to death. After all, if you follow Satan's path, you'll reach Satan's destination.

"In those days, Israel had no king, so the people did whatever seemed right in their own eyes." - Judges 21:25

"If there is no God everything is permitted." – Fyodor Dostoevsky

CHAPTER 3
GOD CIVILISES THE WORLD

I can hear the objections to the previous chapter now.

"How dare you say that only believers in God can be good people! If God is the source of the MORAL LAW and we need him to understand good and evil, and without him we all turn into 'mouldy apples', then why is it that people who reject him are still capable of good deeds? Atheists do good things all the time. People who reject God don't instantly turn into immoral axe murderers! And what about people of other religions who believe in a different god? You get nice people all around the world regardless of their religion. And anyway, religion has been the cause of all the misery in the world! So this theory is rubbish!"

Well, let's explore these objections. Firstly, why is it that godless people don't instantly turn into axe murderers? Why is it that people who don't believe in God can often still be nice people who do good things? We can give four reasons which I will summarise with four C's.

- The **C**onscience
- **C**reation
- **C**ivil Laws
- The Great **C**ommission

Let's now go through them one-by-one.

THE CONSCIENCE

The Bible tells us that God has written His MORAL LAW into the hearts of every human being and that it speaks to everyone through their consciences. Paul writes in Romans that, *"Even when Gentiles, who do not have God's written law, instinctively follow what the law says, they show that in their hearts they know right from wrong. They demonstrate that God's law is written within them, for their own consciences either accuse them or tell them they are doing what's right."* (Rom 2:14-15)

Every single human being in the world has been given a conscience which gives everyone an instinctive sense of right and wrong. We all have this little voice inside our spirits that reminds us of God's MORAL LAW - often when we least want to hear it. In fact, quite often our conscience tells us to do the exact *opposite* of what we'd prefer to do! And the thing is this:

There is no naturalistic or atheistic explanation for the conscience.

Why is it that when we really want to sin...and I mean really, really want to sin...I mean when every part of our mind and body is desperate on some self-gratifying sin...there is still another part of us... a part that seems quite separate...trying to keep us on the straight and narrow? Trying to reign our desires in? Where does that voice come from? Why is it so annoyingly *insistent* that you do the right thing? How can its desires be so different from yours? Where does this inner conflict come from?

There's this moral arbiter sitting within your spirit convicting you and trying to guide you in the right way. And sometimes you don't want to listen to it. Sometimes it frustrates you. Sometimes you wish it wasn't there. Because it's bothering you and telling you that you're wrong. It's reminding you of the MORAL LAW. And you hate that. Why can't it just leave you alone to do the self-serving thing? Why is it s determined to frustrate your passions?

That voice that you're hearing, your conscience, is the voice of God within your spirit.

And everyone has one. Everyone has this internal moral arbiter watching over your words and deeds. In times gone by the MORAL LAW was even referred to as the NATURAL LAW or the LAW OF NATURE because knowledge of right and wrong via their conscience was considered natural and instinctive to all human beings. The word "conscience" literally translates as *"with knowledge"*. It's the natural knowledge of right and wrong within your spirit. Put there by God.

And this is reason number one why people who have rejected God don't instantly turn into axe murderers. Their consciences act as a restraint on their selfish desires.

CREATION

Secondly, the Bible tells us that God has revealed himself to everyone, everywhere, through His creation. *"For the truth about God is known to them instinctively. God has put this knowledge in their hearts. From the time the world was created, people have seen the earth and sky and all that God made. They can clearly see his invisible qualities — his eternal power and divine nature. So they have no excuse whatsoever for not knowing God."* (Rom 1:19-20)

It's beyond the scope of this book to explore in detail how God has revealed himself through creation but it doesn't take a PhD in science to look around and see the diversity, beauty, complexity and magnitude of the world and conclude that there must be an amazing creator behind it all. Creation informs us of the Creator in the exact same way that a building informs us of the builder and a painting informs us of the painter. Just as you can get insight into the person of Van Gogh by looking at one of Van Gogh's paintings, you can get insight into God by looking at God's creation. Nature reflects who God is and speaks to us about His character.

In this sense, God's design for creation automatically acts as a restraint on our moral conduct by demanding our co-operation with it.

For example, if we want to have babies, creation says that can only happen one way - between one man and one woman. If we try to go against creation and pro-create within same sex partnerships, we are wasting our time. It just can't happen. So we are forced by the design of God's creation, which reflects His character, to have natural sexual relations if we want to have a family and there is no other option. Creation is informing us of the Creator here and coercing our co-operation.

Indeed, whenever we act against our natural design or the natural order of creation, we tend to find there is a significant price to pay. If we drink excessively our body gets hangovers which make us feel rotten. If we persist we even get liver disease. If we consistently eat more than our bodies need out of selfish greed we become obese and develop health problems. If we look to selfishly sleep around we feel tremendous emotional pain, guilt and feelings of worthlessness. We may also pick up sexually transmitted infections. Homosexuality is notoriously disease-ridden. Drug taking damages the brain and can lead to death. So again, if we want to stay healthy and happy, we are forced to co-operate with creation. We are forced to co-operate with God's design. In that sense, creation informs us of the MORAL LAW and restricts us from falling into complete 'do what you want' selfishness. God speaks to us constantly through what He has made.

I also love the quote by Abraham Lincoln where he said, *"I can see how it might be possible for a man to look down upon the earth and be an atheist, but I cannot conceive how he could look up into the heavens and say there is no God."*

Creation tells us that there most be some meaning to all this. We instinctively know it.

CIVIL LAWS

Thirdly, human beings are smart enough to know that society needs a moral code to function so generally speaking God's MORAL LAW is upheld by the civil law of the land. For example, the MORAL LAW says murder is wrong so in most countries the civil law says that murder is illegal. If you murder someone the police force will come after you and the judiciary system will make you pay. Obviously that acts as a deterrent to 'do what you want' living.

Likewise, the MORAL LAW says stealing is wrong so in most countries theft will be illegal. In other words, God's voice is heard through the civil laws of the land which are upheld and enforced by the human authorities. In that sense the government and civil authorities of a nation actually do God's bidding. Even though we may want to 'do what we want', we are informed, restrained and penalised by the civil law. And this is reason number 3 why we don't all immediately become fantastically immoral without God.

This is especially pertinent when we consider that many nations, particularly those subscribing to English Common Law, have actually built their constitutions and legal systems upon Biblical principles. So pervasive has the influence of Christianity been, that the Bible has historically been *foundational* to our sense of civil justice.

THE GREAT COMMISSION

The fourth reason why people around the world have a general adherence to the MORAL LAW regardless of their esteem for the Creator, is because of Jesus' last command to Christians before He ascended to heaven: *"go and make disciples of all the nations, baptizing them in the name of the Father and the Son and the Holy Spirit. Teach these new disciples to obey all the commands I have given you. And be sure of this: I am with you always, even to the end of the age."* (Matt 28:19-20)

This is known as the Great Commission.

Jesus left His followers the task of going into the world spreading the gospel message, and this they were to do diligently until the day of His return (Matt 24:14). Because many Christians have taken this commission so seriously, there have, for the past 2000 years, been people going into every corner of the world teaching, evangelising, witnessing and going on missionary journeys. Consequently Christian morality has spread far and wide and has civilised and influenced the world in more ways than it realises or would want to acknowledge. I think it's worth going into some detail on this.

Infanticide

For example, in almost all cultures prior to the arrival of Christianity the killing of babies, known as infanticide, was a common practice. According to researchers Susan Scrimshaw and James Dennis, it was the norm in Greco-Roman culture, in India, China, Japan, Brazil, pagan Africa, amongst the Indians of North and South America and the Eskimos. Babies particularly at risk were the deformed, disabled or just the female - in ancient cultures male babies were more prized than female ones so in Greece for example, it was rare for even a wealthy family to raise more than one daughter. An ancient inscription at Delphi in Greece states that in the 2nd century only 1% of families there raised more than one daughter. Disabled babies were simply seen as sub-human and were drowned.

In many pagan cultures babies were also killed as a form of sacrifice to pagan gods like Baal and Asherah. Near Mount Carmel in the area of Megiddo, archaeologists have discovered the remains of infants who, under the corrupt reign of King Ahab and Queen Jezebel in 9BC, had been sacrificed in a temple of Asherah. This was very typical in pagan cultures.

The pre-Christian Irish were well known to be into this behaviour and the Lithuanians and Prussians carried out child sacrifice right up until the 14th Century. British author Edward Ryan says that they, *"would have done so to this day were it not for Christianity."* Druidic forms of paganism were particularly nasty on this front. And the same thing went on in Aztec and Mayan culture.

It was the spread of Christianity through European settlers that led to the outlawing of all types of infanticide. Christianity taught a new message that claimed that all human life contained the image of God and therefore all were equally valuable.

Child Abandonment

Babies that weren't killed in Greco Roman culture were often just abandoned. Euripides, the Greek poet from 5BC, mentions infants being thrown into rivers and manure piles, exposed on road sides, and left for prey to birds and wild animals. Greek and Roman literature is full of stories of abandoned children and in Sparta, when any child was born, it had to be taken before the tribal elders who would then decide whether the child should be kept or thrown away. It was Christians like Clement of Alexandria and Tertullian who were pioneers in the campaign against these atrocities.

Indeed, Christians didn't just protest against these practices but were also willing to go the extra mile and proactively set about caring for abandoned children by establishing orphanages, foster homes and drop off points at churches. We take such institutions for granted now but these were brand new Christian initiatives at the time. Callistus was known for finding homes for abandoned children and Benigus of Dijon provided protection and nourishment for children, some of whom were deformed by failed abortions. Efforts by Christians like these helped change worldviews and eventually led to the outlawing of child abandonment.

Abortion

It was Christians that changed attitudes towards abortion which was also prevalent in Greco Roman culture.

Respect and honour for marriage dwindled until it became almost extinct in Roman times. Latterly, faithful women were said by the Roman poet Juvenal to be non-existent. As the women slept around they inevitably became pregnant and as they became pregnant they inevitably needed to dispose of the 'evidence' of their unfaithfulness - this meant abortion rates went through the roof (a rise in sexual promiscuity in any culture will always be paid for by the blood of the resulting babies.) And in Roman times, human life was cheap and expendable. Therefore, even philosophers of the era like Plato, Aristotle and Celsus and still others well after Christ had no compunctions about taking the life of an unborn child.

It was Christians that stood against the culture of the day to unequivocally condemn it. The Christian Athenagoras wrote to the Roman Emperor Marcus Aurelius to express his outrage at the practice. Tertullian also spoke of the Christian position when he said, *"We may not destroy even the foetus in the womb...nor does it matter whether you take away the life that is born or destroy one that is coming from birth."*(Apology 9) As historian WEH Lecky says, *"the value and sanctity of infant life...broadly distinguished Christian from Pagan societies."* There was a marked contrast between Christians and the culture around them and it was the Christians who civilised the world.

Sanctity of Adult Life

Adult life was cheap and expendable to the Greeks and Romans too. Gladiatorial shows where humans killed each other for entertainment was the norm. Each contest required men to fight other men and often animals too. The barbaric cruelty, the agonising screams of the victims, and the flow of human blood stirred no conscience in the crowd who cheered and bayed for more slaughter. In contrast, Christians were appalled by this gambling with human life. They boycotted it and condemned it. This too brought them into conflict with the pagan Romans.

Minicuis Felix cites a Roman pagan who strongly criticised Christians for their anti-gladitorial stance saying, *"You do not go to our shows; you take no part in our processions...you shrink in horror from our sacred gladitorial games."* The Romans hated these Christians who wouldn't join in and go with the cultural flow. Eventually as Jerome Carcopino says, *"the butcheries of the arena were stopped at the command of Christian emperors."* Lecky concurs saying, *"There is scarcely any single reform so important in the moral history of mankind as the suppression of the gladiatorial shows, a feat that must be almost exclusively ascribed to the Christian church."*

Suicide

It was Christians who changed attitudes towards suicide which was seen as honourable and romantic in Roman and some Asian cultures amongst others.

Cannibalism

It was Christian missionaries who ended cannibalism in many tribal cultures around the world too. There is the anecdotal story of a communist explorer who encountered a jungle tribe and did proceed to warn them about Christianity and its missionaries. *"If any should ever come this way don't listen to their fairytales"*, was his message. The tribal chief listened intently to his tirade and then explained to the communist that he should be very glad of those missionaries whom he hates and warns against, for some had actually passed through their camp some time ago and if they hadn't done so, the tribe would have eaten him by now - as was their custom before the missionaries brought them the gospel. The Christian influence that had gone before had civilised the tribe, ended cannibalism, and saved the atheist's life.

And that is a microcosmic picture of what has happened in the world at large. As Christianity has spread it has civilised the world. The atheists that follow enjoy the benefits of that civilising effect and have been influenced by it but yet speak against its source.

Marriage

The complete debasement of marriage may have been a problem in Greco Roman culture but it was the spread of Christianity that restored the value, dignity and sanctity of marriage between one man and one woman. In doing so, Christianity helped establish the building blocks of stable and prosperous society.

Paedophilia

It was also Christians who opposed and ended the acceptance and practice of paedophilia, which was a cultural norm in Greco Roman society. In fact, so engrained was this practice into their culture that even the Emperors had these abhorrent relationships. Nero had at least two boys called Sporus and Pythagoras. Sporus was sickeningly castrated so that he could assume the role of 'wife' for Nero. Nero's successor was Galba and he had at least one male lover. Emperor Hadrian had a young boy called Antinuous and Emperor Commodus, along with his three hundred concubines, also had three hundred young boys on staff to satisfy his sexual appetite. Christianity was responsible for opposing this and changing the cultural norms. It was also Christians who opposed homosexuality in general, which was increasingly common in Greco Roman society.

Women

It was Christians who first changed attitudes to women. Apart from the regular killing of baby girls, women in general were deprived of basic freedoms in Greco Roman times.

In India's Hindu culture, when a man died his wife was expected to climb onto his funeral pyre and be burned alive along with him. A practice called *suttee* or *sati*. In contrast, Christianity was teaching the world that widows should be cared for in their old age and it was British authorities, because of an embedded Christian influence, who eventually outlawed suttee. Again, Christianity civilised the world.

In the Q'uran women were, and still are, given half the value of men (4:11), can be used how they want by men (2:223) and can be taken as sex slaves by men (4:24 & 33:50) whereas it was through Christianity that women were given equal value. As Galatians 3:28 says, *"There is no longer Jew or Gentile, slave or free, male and female. For you are all one in Christ Jesus."* This set a precedent for the equality of men and women and the New Testament reports many women who had influential roles in the early church. Phoebe as a deacon, Priscilla was described as a co-worker in Paul's ministry, Lydia, Lois and Eunice are given special mentions and there are many more heroines in the

Bible, even from Old Testament times such as Esther and Deborah.

That contrasting attitude meant that while women were liberated wherever Christianity spread, others in pagan cultures remained enslaved...sometimes even to this day. Look at where Christianity has had most influence and then correlate it with where women have the most freedom. I'm sure you will not be surprised to see the connection. It was also Christian missionaries who led the campaign to abolish things like foot-binding of women in China. Before Christianity, little or no dignity was given to women at all.

Charities & Social Justice

It was Christians who initiated the modern idea of charity – that is, giving that expected nothing in return. In Greco Roman culture, giving would be done either to gain favour with someone or to place someone in your debt so you could call in a favour at a later date. Christianity taught giving for giving's sake because it was Jesus that said, *"it is more blessed to give than to receive."* (Also see Luke 14:12-14) It was Christ's revolutionary teaching to love our enemies that meant *everyone* received Christian charity; foes as well as friends. That kindness often wasn't repaid.

Where the Stoic philosophy of Roman culture had made it disrespectful to associate with the weak, poor and downtrodden, Christians regarded all individuals as having equal value no matter what their social status. They were happy to associate with society's underclass, just as Jesus had done. It was Christians who therefore founded orphanages. It was Christians who first established homes for the aged. It was Christians, specifically working on Christian principles, like

Anthony Ashley Cooper, that introduced child labour laws. Cooper wrote about his motivation as a young man saying, *"I want nothing but usefulness to God and my country."* Again, if we look to places where Christianity has had less influence, we see child labour still in effect, even today. Carlton Hayes said, *"From the wellsprings of Christian compassion, our Western civilisation has drawn its inspiration, and sense of duty, for feeding the hungry, giving drink to the thirsty, looking after the homeless, clothing the naked, tending the sick, and visiting the prisoner."*

Before Christianity, there was nothing that we would recognise today as hospitals. The idea of nursing the sick was largely a Christian one. For example, history records three plagues that hit Rome known as the Antonine Plague, Cyprian Plague and Justinian Plague. Historians note that these dark periods were when Christianity experienced its largest surges in growth. Why? Because while pagan Romans abandoned their sick according to their custom and for fear of catching it themselves, Christians had a casual disregard for death and cared for the sick in their own communities *and* in pagan communities – once more showing love for those who hated them. This meant that Christians themselves had a far higher survival rate and it also meant pagan survivors, moved by seeing faith in action, converted to Christianity. This was revolutionary.

Look towards the origin of most charitable organisations today, particularly of the oldest variety, and you'll discover they are normally always rooted in Christianity too. Where Christians have pioneered, others have followed. I recommend that you do some research into this claim yourself.

Education

Christians were the first to believe in formally educating both men *and* women. WM Ramsay says that Christianity's aim was, *"universal education, not education confined to the rich, as among the Greeks and Romans...and it made no distinction of sex."* This was a radical concept. Prior to Christianity, education was generally for the rich and for the male only. Christianity changed things.

It was Martin Luther, the Christian reformer, who first suggested the idea of tax supported public schools so everyone, rich and poor, could receive a free education. Although public schools have now become totally secularised and God isn't allowed in many of them these days, they were in fact a Christian innovation.

It was a Christian, Johann Sturm who introduced the idea of graded education. A Christian, Friedrich Froebel, instigated the kindergarten concept. It was people like Abbe Charles Michel de l'Epee, Thomas Galludet and Laurent Clerc who created sign language simply motivated by the fact that deaf people should be able to hear the gospel of Jesus. Christians initiated education for the blind. Louis Braille, who created the Braille system that allowed the blind to read, saw his work as a divine mission. When the poor didn't take advantage of free education, Robert Raikes started the idea of Sunday School so that everyone could receive at least some kind of instruction one day a week.

In the United States, every American college founded in the colonies prior to the Revolutionary War – except the University of Pennsylvania – was established by a self-identified branch of the Christian church. Even by 1932, 92% of the 182 colleges and universities in America were founded by self-identified Christian denominations. That is, a body claiming to represent and be moved by faith in Christ. Again, God isn't welcome in some of them anymore, but they wouldn't have existed without Christians being motivated by their faith to create a better world. The world now enjoys the benefits but hates the source of the benefits.

Slavery & Racism

And then finally, who could forget Christians like William Wilberforce, who spent his whole life fighting to abolish the slave trade in the British Empire. As the first to achieve this goal, he opened up the path for the same thing to happen around the world and millions of people from that day forth were spared the horror and indignity of slavery.

Or what about the Baptist preacher, Martin Luther King Jr., who was the first to take a real stand for racial equality in the USA and who changed the attitudes of a nation by peaceful means because of his commitment to Christian principles. Luther King Jr. stood in contrast to the Muslim, Malcolm X, who had no hesitation in advocating violence, anti-Semitism and racism for his cause.

We haven't really scratched the surface of how the message of Christ has changed the world via His followers and I've skimmed over the details for the sake of brevity. So no wonder historian Kenneth Scott Latourette said, *"As the centuries pass, the evidence is accumulating that, measured by his effect on history, Jesus is the most influential life ever lived on this planet."*

HG Wells wrote, *"I am an historian, I am not a believer, but I must confess as a historian that this penniless preacher from*

Nazareth is irrevocably the very centre of history. Jesus Christ is easily the most dominant figure in all history."

James C Hefley wrote, *"I am within the mark when I say that all the armies that ever marched, and all the navies that were ever built, and all the parliaments that ever sat, and all the kings that ever reigned, put together, have not affected the life of man upon earth as powerfully as has that One Solitary Life."*

If Jesus had never lived, and if His followers hadn't been so committed to the cause of putting faith into action, spreading the gospel like they have, the world would never have eradicated all the evils described above.

Kenneth L. Woodward, writing in Newsweek, said, *"Because Christianity's influence is so pervasive throughout much of the world, it is easy to forget how radical its beliefs once were."*

And that's exactly it. Christianity once seemed radical because it looked totally different to the evil cultures into which it entered. Like a midday sky compared to a midnight sky. But gradually, through its followers, Christianity changed those cultures and created new moral norms. Christianity slowly made the world brighter. People now take the light by which we live for granted, forgetting the place from where it came. But look into this issue in any depth and you will quickly find that Christianity has been the driving force of civilisation for over two thousand years. Indeed, it continues to civilise the world and bring dignity, hope and freedom wherever it goes today - whether that be with jungle tribes or city streets.

Take the Street Pastors initiative for example, where Christian volunteers look to bring Christ into the city centres of Great Britain. They go out onto the streets at night, particularly to city centres where lost and broken people are stumbling out of bars drunk, upset and getting into fights. On 23rd April, 2010, BBC News reported that in Northamptonshire, England, alone, police recorded a 65.5% reduction in crime on the previous year as a direct result of this Christian influence on the streets. You'll find roughly the same figures in every town where Street Pastors operates.

In the year 2000, the Social Capital Community Benchmark Survey (SCCBS) was undertaken by the universities of the USA and it discovered that if two people – one religious and one atheist – are identical in every other way - economically, socially and politically – the atheist is 23% less likely to give to charity and 26% less likely to volunteer their time to good causes. (http://www.hoover.org/publications/policy-review/article/6577) God civilises people.

Here is a map released by Transparency International showing national corruption levels. Yellow signifies the least corrupt countries and red signifies the most corrupt.

Although there are many factors to take into consideration, just a quick glance at the map reveals that the least corrupt nations are those with a Christian heritage. I will list the top ten *least* corrupt nations from 2011 along with the predominant religion, as given by the ARDA (Association of Religion Data Archives). New Zealand (70.6% Christian), Denmark (85% Christian), Finland (90.2% Christian), Sweden (64.8% Christian), Singapore (39.2% Chinese Universalist), Norway (91.3% Christian), Netherlands (64% Christian), Australia (74.4% Christian), Switzerland (82.6% Christian), Canada (74.5% Christian), Luxembourg (90.6% Christian), Hong Kong (54.6% Chinese Universalist).

Now even though these percentages represent nominal figures - that is to say, there is no chance that there are that many genuine Christians in those countries today - the percentages shows how the residual historical influence of Christianity is still being felt in those countries. It's still benefiting them, even after they have largely turned away from God. The echo of God's voice is still being heard.

It is simply no coincidence that corruption has fallen wherever Christianity has had most historical influence. Even the two anomalies, Hong Kong and Singapore, can perhaps be explained by the fact they once had a strong Christian influence in their days as British colonies.

Language

There is even a lesson to be learned from the way we speak.

When we say we have *'given up the ghost'*, or talk about being *'the salt of the earth'*, or talk about *'putting words into each* other's mouths' or being *'a law unto yourself'* or talk about *'a little bird telling me'* a secret, we are actually quoting the Bible.

The King James Bible in particular is widely regarded to be the most influential book on the English language of all time - even more influential than the works of Shakespeare - and the Bible is also the best-selling book of all time.

The Word of God has gone round the globe bringing light to anyone who reads it and its historical influence is seen in the fact that non-believers use these phrases from the Bible, without knowing that's where they originated. And that is a perfect example of a much bigger truth - that the world has been influenced by Biblical morals without knowing that they originated with God.

Slavery is a perfect example. It was once very much embedded in culture and no one thought anything of it. It took William Wilberforce - a Christian, driven by Christ, working to Christian principles, giving his whole life to the fight - to change the culture and set a new norm. Today slavery is considered a self-evident evil and the fact that its abolition was a primarily Christian accomplishment is totally forgotten. Instead, people vainly imagine that we have achieved moral progress by some natural evolutionary force. Nothing could be further from the truth. Christians fulfilling the Great Commission gave their lives to establish those advances.

So the truth of the matter is that although atheists and many others around the world won't acknowledge it, they hold many of their best moral opinions simply because they have inherited and internalised truths that Christians had to fight to establish as cultural norms. It is because of Christian pioneers that Christian principles have permeated the atmosphere of our society. Pioneers like Paul of Tarsus, Wilberforce, Luther, Luther King Jr. and all those before and after them who revolutionised the inferior social morality of their time and set new standards.

As Fyodor Dostoyevsky said, *"Even those who have renounced Christianity and attack it, in their inmost being still follow the Christian ideal."* They have just forgotten that it's from Christ that those ideals came.

Yet our knowledge of right and wrong inextricably comes from God.

CHAPTER 4
THE ENTROPY OF SIN

Well then, if we instinctively follow the MORAL LAW because God has given us a conscience, creation demands our co-operation, and we have internalised Christian values from godly pioneers obeying the great commission, and civil laws keep us on track anyway, then why are things still crumbling?

Well it goes back to our sinful human hearts again. Our terrible natural condition. Remember Jesus said, *"For from the heart come evil thoughts, murder, adultery, all sexual immorality, theft, lying and slander. These are what defile you."* (Matt 15:19-20)

It goes back to the fact that in our very core we have this selfish, sinful nature that wants to gratify itself. It wants to ignore the conscience, creation's design, civil laws and gospel preaching of the great commission and it wants to do its own thing. What it wants is to sin. And that's where all the problems on earth begin.

THE LAW OF ENTROPY

There's a law at work in the universe called the 2nd Law of Thermodynamics, or the Law of Entropy. It applies to everything in creation and it basically states that the natural tendency of the universe is towards disorder rather than order. Towards devolution rather than evolution. When you leave things to themselves, they ultimately decay, disintegrate, decompose, or die.

One of the best ways to picture this law in action is to imagine building a sand castle in the desert. As you build your castle, you will temporarily bring order and structure to the grains of sand that surround you. You will introduce order and form into the chaos. However, if you then leave that sand castle to the natural elements, the wind will start to erode the castle and the order will be destroyed. After enough time has passed, what was once a structured sandcastle will become a chaotic, formless mound of sand again.

Everything in the universe is subject to this natural tendency from order to chaos. It's why mortar crumbles, glass shatters, clothes become threadbare and buildings collapse. It's why there's such a thing as a DIY industry. Ultimately it's why we age and die. We're always having to repair, repaint or replace things that are breaking apart and disintegrating. It takes a lot of effort to maintain order and structure.

Now this applies to our moral condition too. If we want to maintain or create moral order within our hearts we need to constantly nourish them and reinforce them. They need to be constantly regenerated. If that doesn't happen, they will start to automatically degenerate. It happens like an apple turning mouldy. We rot gradually within.

When left to ourselves, our natural tendency towards selfishness and sin will pull us into ever darker places. We will decay into moral disorder and chaos. The law of entropy will take our hearts.

Let's go back through the 4 C's to see how our concept of morality can be eroded over a period of time when we reject God.

CONSCIENCE

Firstly, we learned that every person in the world has a conscience that informs them of the MORAL LAW. This internal moral arbiter tries to keep all of us on the straight and narrow.

However, the Bible makes it clear that when we consistently disobey God by ignoring that conscience and choosing to go our own selfish way instead, our conscience becomes seared. This means it becomes calloused, hardened or insensitive. The Bible frequently refers to people 'hardening their hearts' against God and that's what it means. Some translations of the Bible even refer to the death of the conscience (1 Tim 4:2). It becomes either severely desensitised or completely incapable of discerning right and wrong. And the more that happens, the less power it has to restrain people from 'do what you want' living and the more likely people are to become cruel, selfish and capable of extreme acts of violence and wickedness.

When we reject God and choose our own path, that is our natural inner trajectory. We become desensitised to evil and accept it as normal. Our hearts become harder. Remember what we learned before. When a man is getting better he understands more and more clearly the evil that is still left in him. When a man is getting worse, he understands his own badness less and less.

Be honest with yourself. Is there something you freely do now which your conscience once bothered you about? Something where, the first time you had the opportunity to do it you hesitated? You knew it wasn't right. You wrestled with it. But then you forged ahead and did it anyway? And then you kind of got into the habit of doing it. And as you got into the habit of it the inner voice of opposition weakened. And now you don't hear the voice at all anymore. You hardly think twice these days and it seems kind of normal and acceptable. Drugs? Porn addiction? Sleeping with your boyfriend outside marriage? Certain movies you watch? Music you listen to with blasphemous lyrics? Have you de-sensitised yourself to your conscience and convinced yourself that what you're doing is ok? Have you created loopholes for yourself and bent the MORAL LAW to suit yourself?

In hardening your conscience so that you can pursue your own path, you have created a way to do what you want but you've inflicted a kind of damage on your spirit. And as people in general do this same thing for the cause of of self-gratification, the cumulative effect of the desensitisation is an increasingly cold and loveless society. We're witnessing the mass desensitisation of conscience in our world today. People are now capable of shocking deeds.

Remember we can develop hardened hearts though our environment and experiences too.

What do you absorb? What entertains you? What do you watch? What do you listen to? What do you worship?

Children are growing up in a culture now where they constantly absorb all kinds of evil through video games, television, internet, music, magazines etc. They're exposed to violence, perversion, sexual sin and wickedness from a much earlier age and it's rotting their souls and hardening their hearts. What was once shocking and morally repulsive is now considered the norm.

I remember when a lesbian kiss was screened on British television for the first time and it created a national outcry. Now it happens all the time without raising an eyebrow. In fact, it's welcomed.

Pop culture feeds a steady stream of garbage into our souls and constantly looks to plumb new depths so as to be more shocking and more explicit. Moral entropy comes by small degrees and our conscience becomes numbed with each step.

I always think the music industry is a great example of this. When Elvis came on the scene in the 1950s people were shocked by him. Now we look at Elvis and can't imagine how anyone so harmless could have once been so controversial. This is because Elvis opened the door for the Beatles who opened the door for Led Zeppelin who opened the door for Black Sabbath who opened the door for Marilyn Manson, Eminem and Cradle of Filth etc. and now we've reached a stage where mainstream pop stars aimed at pre-teen children dress like porn stars and sing openly about drugs and sex. And parents, not understanding the damage it's inflicting on their child's hearts, approve of it.

Today, from this place of cultural darkness, Elvis looks like a saint by comparison, just as a 5am sky looks bright to those living in midnight darkness. What happened is that our parents rebelled against their parent's standards and set a new low. Our generation then used those lowered standards as our starting point and rebelled against them too. Our kids will then take our standards and lower them further. Society keeps getting darker. Pushing moral boundaries. Knocking down walls of taste and decency and purity and innocence.

We're strangely baffled by the toll this is taking on our children's souls. On November 3rd, 2011, a survey by the children's charity, Barnardos discovered that almost half of adult Britons already thought that children in Great Britain were feral and starting to behave like animals. This is just external evidence of internal corruption. This is simply what happens when God is rejected and moral entropy takes effect. The inner moral compass is lost and people start to do what they please instead. And this is just the next generation. What will their kids or grandkids look like unless the entropy is brought to a halt?

And then we have the hardening of hearts through personal experiences too. People are increasingly living in a world of divorce, fatherless families, rejection, isolation, distrust, bitterness and greed. People are becoming emotionally injured and they're injuring others. The cancer is spreading.

Finally, it must be noted that the conscience is contained within the spirit which is the part of the human that can be demonised. So for example, when people get involved in heavy occultism their consciences can be interfered with and instead of the voice of God, people can hear the demonic voice of evil instead. Unfortunately, occultism is on the rise in our culture through things like Eastern religion, astrology, yoga, reiki and necromancy.

Do you think people are become more callous? Less warm? Less forthcoming? Are our towns and city streets less safe for our kids than when we were young? Do you look back a decade or two with nostalgia because those days seemed more innocent somehow? This is what happens to society without it's moral reference point.

CREATION

Secondly, we saw that people are informed about the truth of God through creation and to a certain extent they must co-operate with its design if they're to stay happy and healthy. But people can deliberately choose to harden themselves to the truth about God from what they see in creation too. Paul explains what happens as a result:

"But God shows his anger from heaven against all sinful, wicked people who suppress the truth by their wickedness. They know the truth about God because he has made it obvious to them. For ever since the world was created, people have seen the earth and sky. Through everything God made, they can clearly see his invisible qualities—his eternal power and divine nature. So they have no excuse for not knowing God.

Yes, they knew God, but they wouldn't worship him as God or even give him thanks. And they began to think up foolish ideas of what God was like. As a result, their minds became dark and confused. Claiming to be wise, they instead became utter fools. And instead of worshiping the glorious, ever-living God, they worshiped idols made to look like mere people and birds and animals and reptiles.

So God abandoned them to do whatever shameful things their hearts desired. As a result, they did vile and degrading things with each other's bodies. They traded the truth about God for a lie. So they worshiped and served the things God created instead of the Creator himself, who is worthy of eternal praise! Amen. That is why God abandoned them to their shameful desires. Even the women turned against the natural way to have sex and instead indulged in sex with each other. And the men, instead of having normal sexual relations with women, burned with lust for each other. Men did shameful things with other men, and as a result of this sin, they suffered within themselves the penalty they deserved.

Since they thought it foolish to acknowledge God, he abandoned them to their foolish thinking and let them do things that should never be done. Their lives became full of every kind of wickedness, sin, greed, hate, envy, murder, quarreling, deception, malicious behavior, and gossip. They are backstabbers, haters of God, insolent, proud, and boastful. They invent new ways of sinning, and they disobey their parents. They refuse to understand, break their promises, are heartless, and have no mercy. They know God's justice requires that those who do these things deserve to die, yet they do them anyway. Worse yet, they encourage others to do them, too." - Romans 1:18-32

Paul says that when people ignore the truth about God they fall into wicked perversion. Notice how he focuses on sexual perversion in particular here. One of the basic moral truths that God tells us through creation is that men and women were created for one another. Just by observing creation alone, this should be blatantly obvious. I don't want to get too explicit but if we had no knowledge of God at all and simply saw a naked man and woman next to one another or had even a basic understanding of biology, we would logically deduce that these two different types of beings were meant for one another. Procreation is only possible between men and women - God is speaking through creation there.

And not only are they clearly physically compatible but further observation would show them to be mentally and emotionally compatible too. Their natural attributes and desires are complementary. You would pick all this up just by an honest appraisal of creation itself.

Therefore, it is deliberate suppression of the obvious truth to go against this natural order and to insist that homosexuality is natural or normal too. When we wilfully suppress the truth like this, our minds become dark and confused. We begin indulging in selfish, sinful behaviour and our morality goes into tailspin. We get into Satan's 'do what you want' philosophy. That's the kind of thing Paul is getting at in this passage. And that's what we're seeing in the world today.

Even though creation coerces us to co-operate with it because we suffer if we go against our design, the truth is, over time our will-power and self-restraint can become so broken down, our hearts can become so polluted, and our selfish desires can become so strong, that we're willing to suffer any amount of pain, even to the point of self-destruction, rather than give up our vice. (Prov 25:28)

People smoke knowing it's going to kill them but they can't stop. People drink alcohol to excess knowing it's going to give them hangovers but they do it anyway. They know the risks of liver disease yet they can't resist. They eat and can't stop despite the health problems. They know they'll regret the sexual encounter in the morning and understand it can lead to disease and accidental pregnancies. Yet the lust for selfish satisfaction begins to override all restraints. They take drugs because they just don't care anymore. They contract HIV willingly because it will let them continue in their homosexual lifestyle with no further restraints. "Do what you want" leads to our own destruction because we go against creation's natural design.

The Bible calls this becoming a slave to sin (John 8:34). You don't really free yourself when you disregard God at all. And Satan's path isn't liberty. It's death. You become a slave to your destructive desires. Desires which, without restraint, will lead to disease, jealousy, distrust and destruction. It's God who, in fact, gives you the power to be liberated from those things which will ultimately destroy you.

We'll talk more about that later.

CIVIL LAWS

Thirdly, we saw that nations base their civil laws on the MORAL LAW for social cohesion and so the voice of God is heard through those human authorities.

But it's also true to say that civil laws can be changed. And constitutions can be amended.

In fact laws can be changed so often that in due course they may start to deviate dramatically from their Biblical foundation. You see, what's legal and what's morally right isn't always the same thing. Everything Adolf Hitler did in Germany was legal and everything Oskar Schindler did was illegal. The laws of Nazi Germany were changed to permit evil and criminalise good. That can happen.

So when God is marginalised from society and the moral reference point is lost, we tend to find a divergence between the MORAL LAW and the civil law. As our minds become darker and morally confused, our law-makers lose sight of what good and evil is and change laws to permit depravity.

Where Christianity's influence once led to the outlawing of abortion, that has now been reversed and is legal again in many countries. Where Christianity's influence once led to the illegalisation of homosexuality, it's now legal. In fact, we've even seen the legalisation of homosexual 'marriage'. Safeguards against euthanasia are now being broken down along with respect for widows and the elderly. Many so-called experts have recently been calling for the legalisation of soft drugs. On March 3rd, 2012, two medical ethicists even called for the re-legalisation of infanticide. That call caused revulsion amongst the public at the time but in 5 years, maybe 10 years, maybe 15, the moral entropy is going to bring the world to a position where infanticide will not only be accepted, but it will be normal.

I say that prophetically but not by any special revelation; I know it simply by observing and learning from history. Without God we decay. All the evils that were once vanquished by the spread of Christianity are now creeping back in. Claiming to be enlightened, people have instead become foolish and confused and civil laws have begun to reflect that.

John De Armond said, *"You know your country is dying when you have to make a distinction between what is moral and ethical, and what is legal."*

We have, unfortunately, already arrived at the place where we need to make that distinction.

THE GREAT COMMISSION

And that leads us onto the final point: Just as the world was civilised by the spread of the Gospel through Christian pioneers, it will just as easily decline without that influence.

This is a simple graph to illustrate the point:

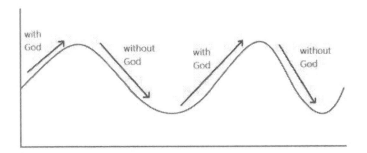

Read through the Book of Kings 1 & 2 in the Bible and you'll see this pattern in action. When Israel was ruled by a good king who brought them close to God they prospered but when they were ruled by a bad king who led them away from God, they decayed.

Judge, writer and historian, Alexander Tytler, famously observed this phenomenon from secular history too. He said,

"The world's great civilizations have progressed through this sequence: From bondage to spiritual faith; from spiritual faith to great courage; from courage to liberty; from liberty to abundance; from abundance to selfishness; from selfishness to complacency; from complacency to apathy; from apathy to dependence; from dependence back again into bondage."

If we turn his observations into a simple graph again, it looks like this:

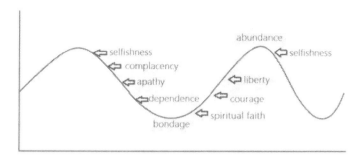

Tytler says that the pivotal point that leads a nation out of bondage is spiritual faith. In other words, the ascent begins with God. As soon as spiritual faith comes into the hearts of men and women, we get an increase in courage, liberty and abundance.

He then notes how the pivotal moment towards decay begins with selfishness. That is to say, doing what I want, defining my own truth, apart from God. The path of Satan. It leads us back into bondage.

And these are the only two paths we have. Follow God and flourish; follow Satan and decay. That's the choice we have ahead of us.

As society abandons God we will see gradually the sanctity of life diminishing, meaning we'll see an increase in senseless violence, killing, abortion, infanticide and child abandonment. We will start to see marriage devalued and sexual promiscuity rise. Homosexuality will, and already is, becoming an accepted social norm once again. Paedophilia will increase. Selfishness will increase and inequality between people will rise. Corruption will increase. Exploitation and poverty will increase. The elderly and widows, instead of being respected, will be disregarded as an irrelevant nuisance.

We will regress. The law of entropy within our hearts will cause our decay.

We see it happening even now.

And all the while, because we're losing sight of the Absolute Light, we'll stop being able to understand our own darkness. We'll call this regression, 'progress'. We'll call the enslavement of our souls, 'liberty'. We'll call debauchery, 'enlightenment'. We will, in fact, end up in bondage. And we'll hate the God who could save us from our own destruction because we'll believe Satan's lies that His moral law is a tyranny.

THE FAILED EXPERIMENT

For clear evidence of what happens when a society banishes God altogether, we don't have to look very far into history. The experiment has already been carried out.

T.S Eliot wrote during the 20th Century that, *"The world is trying the experiment of attempting to form a civilized but non-Christian mentality. The experiment will fail..."*

And he was proved correct.

In communist China, Mao Tse-Tung's banned churches and Christian worship. His reign led to the deaths of 37,828,000 people.

The reign of Pol Pot in communist Cambodia led to the infamous killing fields where between 2,397,000 people were wiped out.

Kim Il Sung's communist North Korea led to the deaths of over 3 million civilians and continues to be the most bizarrely oppressive regime in the world under Kim Jong Un.

Joseph Stalin's communist Russia led to the deaths of over 42,672,000 people.

Vladimir Lenin's reign led to the deaths of 4,017,000 people.

Adolf Hitler's socialist Nazi regime led to the horrific concentration camps which killed 6 million Jews and 20,946,000 overall as a result of World War II.

Since many try to paint Hitler as a Christian it's worth pointing out that this is the same Hitler who said in July 1941, *"National Socialism and religion cannot exist together...the heaviest blow that ever struck humanity was the coming of Christianity...[Christianity] is an invention of the Jew. The deliberate lie in the matter of religion was introduced into the world by Christianity." (Bormann 1953, pp.6-7)*

He also said on 14th October, 1941, *"The best thing is to let Christianity die a natural death...when understanding of the universe has become widespread...Christian doctrine will be convicted of absurdity...Christianity has reached the peak of absurdity...And that's why someday its structure will collapse...the only way to get rid of Christianity is to let it die little by little...Christianity is the liar...We'll see to it that the churches cannot spread abroad teachings in conflict with the interests of the state." (Bormann 1953, pp. 49-52)*

Gradually Hitler began to warm to the idea of destroying Christianity himself. On 21st October, 1941 he said, *"By exterminating this pest [Christianity], we shall do humanity a* service of which our soldiers can have no idea." (Bormann 1953, pp.63-65)

Hitler's inner circle agreed. Heinrich Himmler said, "We shall not rest until we have rooted out Christianity." (NAACD 2005)

Wherever God, the reference point of Absolute Good, has been ignored or shut out, people have lost sight of what right and wrong means, have worshipped self and have become brutalised within as the natural sinful human nature runs rampant.

These regimes also prove the point that when you reject worship of God, you automatically end up worshipping self. Man. That's what happened with Tse-Tung, Stalin, Hitler and their like. You reject one path and you automatically end up on the other.

And far from representing a path to liberty, which is how all these regimes initially marketed their ideas, it actually led to moral corruption, oppression and death. This is the natural end of any nation that removes God from His position of authority. This is the natural end of any individual who does likewise. Man will make himself the measure of all things and out of his sinful heart will flow immorality, greed, murder and lies.

When you reject God, you automatically end up worshipping self. Worshipping man. Man becomes god. That's what happened with these God hating, man deifying regimes. And as such, they represent the most morally corrupt and oppressive regimes in world history.

"For from the heart come evil thoughts, murder, adultery, all sexual immorality, theft, lying and slander. These are what defile you." (Matt 15:19-20)

Atheists often try to invert this truth and claim that 'religion' is the cause of all evil in the world. And by religion, they tend to be aiming at Christianity. They say that God is the cause of wars and misery and that to eradicate the notion would bring peace.

Philip & Axelrod actually investigated this when writing the three volume *Encyclopaedia of Wars*. They discovered that out of the 1,763 wars that they could chronicle from human history, 123 were religious in nature. That means only 6.98% of all wars in history have been religious. When those waged in the name of Islam were taken out, that figure was more than halved to 3.23%.

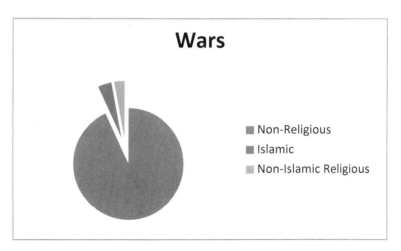

So the evidence again proves that the problem really arises in the *absence* of God.

RJ Rummel spoke of atheistic regimes in his book *Lethal Politics And Death* saying: *"Almost 170 million men, women and* children have been shot, beaten, tortured, knifed, burned, starved, frozen, crushed or worked to death; buried alive, drowned, hung, bombed or killed in any other of a myriad of ways governments have inflicted death on unarmed, helpless citizens and foreigners. The dead could conceivably be nearly 360 million people. It is though our species has been devastated by a modern Black Plague. And indeed it has, but a plague of Power, not germs."

Power. The love of self. Greed. Selfish ambition. That's the problem. And these things flow out from within the human heart itself. And God is the *restraint* to those things.

Abraham Lincoln was a leader who knew the health of his nation depended on the Creator. He famously called a Day of Humiliation, Fasting And Repentance for the United States saying, *"It is the duty of nations…to own their dependence upon the overruling power of God, to confess their sins…with assured hope that genuine repentance will lead to mercy…We have been the recipients of the choicest bounties of Heaven…We have grown in numbers, wealth and power as no other nation has ever grown. But we have forgotten God. We have forgotten the gracious Hand which preserved us in peace, and multiplied and enriched and strengthened us; and we have vainly imagined, in the deceitfulness of our hearts, that all these blessings were produced by some superior wisdom and virtue of our own. Intoxicated with unbroken success, we have become too self-sufficient to feel the necessity of redeeming and preserving grace, too proud to pray to the God that made us! It behooves us then to humble ourselves before the offended Power, to confess our national sins and to pray for…forgiveness."*

Lincoln acknowledged the simple fact that his nation would prosper as long as they gave God his place and would decline as soon as they tried to become self-sufficient.

THE TERMINAL DECLINE

Unfortunately, in our day, we're witnessing a world that refuses to read the Bible and refuses to learn from the mistakes of the past. We're continuing the experiment of trying to create a civilised world without God. And as TS Eliot rightly predicted, it will fail. In fact, the Bible tells us that one day the decline that follows this experiment will become terminal.

As we continue down this road, one day people's hearts will become so hardened by their lust for sin, their minds will become so warped, their laws will become so immoral and God will be so excluded, that the world will become a cruel place to be. As the mass of men follow Satan's creed, they will create a hellish planet, and this will set the scene for the Antichrist.

The Bible describes this period as the Great Tribulation and Jesus says of it, *"...there will be greater anguish than at any time since the world began. And it will never be so great again."* (Matt 24:21) Paul wrote to Timothy saying, *"You should know this, Timothy, that in the last days there will be very difficult times. For people will love only themselves and their money. They will be boastful and proud, scoffing at God, disobedient to their parents, and ungrateful. They will consider nothing sacred. They will be unloving and unforgiving; they will slander others and have no self-control. They will be cruel and hate what is good. They will betray their friends, be reckless, be puffed up with pride, and love pleasure rather than God. They will act religious, but they will reject the power that could make them godly."* (2 Tim 3:1-5)

This is the period of time that will be immediately before Jesus returns. The period we are rapidly hurtling towards...the period of time I humbly suggest that has already begun...where the moral entropy of our sinful natures and our rejection of God will bring us to a point of terminal decline. And at that point, Jesus will return.

Let's pray for the hearts of men and women to turn back to God. Let them remember where the source of their blessing comes from. Let them be able to echo the Psalmist who says, *"Let all that I am praise the Lord; may I never forget the good things he does for me."* - Psalm 103:2

CHAPTER 5
OUR RESPONSIBILITY

So we've established that God is the key to understanding right and wrong. We've established that only He can reverse the moral entropy within sinful human hearts. But the thing is...

Christians are the only ones who know that.

When I interviewed the public about what was going wrong with the world they all blamed a variety of people from teachers, politicians, kids, parents and religious leaders and they all thought that it was down to those individuals to get their act together.

They thought that if politicians could just initiate some new reforms, give some strategic tax breaks, set up some programs; if teachers could just up their game, reduce class sizes, try some new learning techniques; if parents could just keep an eye on their kids more, be stricter with them, keep them entertained; if local government could just throw some money at the issue, that would solve it all.

And in every one of those suggestions, they missed the root of the problem. What they were all advocating was similar to trying to deal with a flooding house by setting up barricades, isolating rooms, bringing in water pumps, getting the neighbours round with buckets and establishing a 24 hour rota...none of them thought about just turning off the kitchen tap. No one thought about just going to the source of the problem.

Get God back into the hearts of men and women and you solve everything else; refuse to go to the root and spend your time dealing with the consequences and eventually the house is going to collapse.

You can change politicians as often as you like, implement new governmental programs, announce educational reforms, vote for the other party, change healthcare policies, introduce tax breaks, invest mountains of money and change any number of laws but society is *still* going to collapse. We simply must get to the heart of the issue - the spiritual cancer of godlessness that leaves the sinful heart unchecked.

Democracies cannot survive unless the majority of people do the right thing when no one is looking.

And without God, people quickly lose sight of what right and wrong even is. The solution in fact, isn't a program; it's a Person. But it must be emphasised, the church are the only ones who know that.

And obviously this places a great deal of responsibility on our shoulders. If we see a world that's collapsing and in Jesus Christ we understand that we have the solution, we then have a responsibility to administer that solution. It's like a doctor who sees a patient with a disease and knows exactly the right drug that would heal that disease. He has a moral responsibility to administer it.

Jesus himself told us to administer it.

Jesus gave us the great commission.

He said, *"Therefore, go and make disciples of all the nations, baptizing them in the name of the Father and the Son and the Holy Spirit. Teach these new disciples to obey all the commands I have given you. And be sure of this: I am with you always, even to the end of the age." (Matt 28:19-20)*

Jesus didn't give the great commission to the government; he gave it to the church. He didn't give the great commission to the judges; he gave it to the church. He didn't give the great commission to the school teachers; he gave it to the church. He didn't give the great commission to the civil servants; he gave it to the church. He gave it to *us.*

We are to be the channel through which people hear about Jesus Christ.

In Chapter 3 we read about how Christianity civilised the world solely because of pioneering men and women who spent their lives putting their faith into action. And out of their efforts came the end of abortion, child abandonment, slavery, inequality, ignorance and much poverty. Those things didn't primarily end because the government produced a great program. They ended because, at the most fundamental level, men and women, with faith in their hearts, did everything they could to spread the Christ-life to others. Sure, they used the tools of government, education, healthcare and all the rest to get the job done, but it began with an understanding that it all depended and centred on God. At the most fundamental level, that's how all civilising progress has ever been made.

That was their great commission and it's still our great commission... it's never been retracted.

WE HAVE BEEN DISTRACTED

Christians especially, I think we've lost sight of this. As I write this book it's an American election year and social media outlets are being flooded with pledges of support for this candidate or that candidate. And I'm talking fanatical support. I'm talking 20 Facebook-posts-a-day support. *"Vote for this guy! This is the hero we need! He's going to put everything right! He's going to turn our country around! He's the only one in which we can trust!"*

I can understand non-Christians being caught up in this fervour for a Messianic human leader but Christians, we should know better. We simply must get out of the habit of thinking that the next president or prime minister or economic policy or tax cut or foreign policy will make everything right in the nation. In the run up to elections it's so common to hear things like, *"vote for this guy because he'll pull our troops out of that war we're in."* Or, *"I'm voting for this guy because he's going to reform the health system."* In fact, I've recently seen people insisting that a president should be voted in simply based on his pledge to lower gas/petrol prices. Gas prices? Really? This is our utmost concern? How could we have missed the point by so much? None of these issues will affect the overall trajectory of your country. None.

At the root of all our problems is 'self'. Our healthcare systems are crippled because people are selfishly eating too much, drinking too much, smoking too much, fornicating too much and not exercising enough. Our self-restraint and discipline is broken down. We're hedonistically gorging ourselves to death. Our economy went down the toilet because of sheer greed. Poverty is perpetuated because of corruption. Wars start because we lust after the natural resources that other countries have. The products we buy are kept artificially expensive because of exploitative price fixing. Marketers lie to people about those products so that they'll be duped into handing over money for them.

What allows people to cheat, manipulate and kill others for profit like this? What is it in a man that would rather spend millions of dollars on a private yacht for himself rather than give the money to buy food for people who will literally die without it? What is it in people that would rather have 5 houses for themselves when others have none? The disease of self is the cancer that's destroying us. And Jesus Christ is the cure.

Let's stop looking to professional bodies to change things; let's stop depending on government to change things; let *us* take the responsibility to change things.

IT WILL COST US

Now if we take our great commission seriously it's going to cost us. Just like it has cost the pioneering Christians of history.

All the disciples except one were martyred. The Christians who opposed the immorality of Greco Roman times were put to death in coliseums. The Bible translators were hunted down and persecuted. Wilberforce was isolated and hated. Luther King Jr was assassinated. I'm not saying you'll necessarily be killed but you *will* experience opposition.

However, Jesus asks us to go nonetheless. He said to his disciples as he sent them out into the world, *"Look, I am sending you out as sheep among wolves."* (Matt 10:16) He said, *"And everyone will hate you because you are my followers."* (Mark 13:13)

Jesus didn't say, *"it's much too dangerous for sheep to go out amongst the wolves so stay here in safety."* Or *"wait until people like you more and are open to the message."* He basically said, *"It's dangerous. You might get hurt. People are going to hate you. You'll be like sheep amongst wolves. Now get out there."*

And because they got out there, they changed the world.

That will always happen.

Christians taking the great commission seriously will always change the world.

I get the feeling that Christians today actually think of themselves as powerless in the face of rampant secularism and occult spirituality. We don't think we can really change things. But that's a lie from Satan himself. When you read the book of Acts in the Bible you are left with the distinct and unavoidable conclusion that the Spirit filled Christians in those days really could not have been stopped. They were an irresistible force in the world. Men and women of God were filled with courage to boldly proclaim the gospel by the power of the Holy Spirit, and the 'gates of hell' just couldn't prevail against it.

History proves that this has always been the way. Whenever the Great Commission has been taken seriously, it has *always* changed the world. And that Great Commission still applies to us. We are *all* called to be Wilberforces and Luther King Jrs and apostle Pauls in our own time. To let our faith embolden us to challenge the prevailing norms of our age, endure the scorn, and to change things for the better. To not conform to the world but to be transformed by the renewing of our mind and to then let that inner transformation impact the world around us. That is what it means to be salt and light! And if we take the command seriously, there is simply nothing on earth that can stop it. Nothing.

The only thing that can get in the way is our own apathy and fear.

Frederic D. Huntington once said, *"It is not scientific doubt, not atheism, not pantheism, not agnosticism, that in our day and in this land is likely to quench the light of the gospel. It is a proud, sensuous, selfish, luxurious, church-going, hollow-hearted prosperity."* Are we ready to reach the world even if it costs us?

We have a job to do. It's going to require effort. It's going to require courage. It's going to require us to pray longer, speak louder, work harder, stand taller and fight harder and it's going to mean persecution and ridicule for his name's sake.

You *will* be hated.

But get out there anyway.

"All that's necessary for evil to triumph is for good men to do nothing." - Edmund Burke

"The world is a dangerous place to live; not because of people who are evil, but because of the people who don't do anything about it."- Albert Einstein

"God save us from living in comfort while sinners are sinking in hell!" - Charles Spurgeon

"Brethren, do something; do something, do something! While societies and unions make constitutions, let us win souls. I pray you, be men of action all of you. Get to work and quit yourselves like men." - Charles Spurgeon

"Enemy-occupied territory - that is what the world is. Christianity is the story of how the rightful king has landed, you might say landed in disguise, and is calling us all to take part in a great campaign of sabotage." - CS Lewis

SECTION 2
CHOOSING THE TRUTH

"Wherever the Spirit of the Lord is, there is freedom."
2 Corinthians 3:17

CHAPTER 6
"THE LAW"

In the first section we explored how it's impossible to *know* the MORAL LAW without God. Our understanding of good and evil completely depends on an understanding of God as an absolute moral reference point. We now need to go on to the next thing - how it's impossible to *choose* the MORAL LAW without God.

You see, *knowing* the law and *choosing* the law are two different things. Once you know that something is wrong, it doesn't necessarily affect your desire to do it.

For example, I have a desire to eat chocolate. If the government decided to make chocolate illegal, the ban wouldn't stop me still wanting to eat it. I would still have a desire for it. That's why alcohol prohibition didn't work in the United states in the 1920s. Making alcohol illegal didn't stop people from wanting to drink it. It didn't change desires. And similarly, knowing the difference between right and wrong doesn't necessarily stop us wanting to *choose* wrong. Knowing the MORAL LAW has no effect on our desires.

Why? Again, because we have inherently sinful hearts that desire power, greed, lust and self-gratification. It doesn't matter what the MORAL LAW says; those desires are there.

So law doesn't have the power to make anyone good. It doesn't have the power to regenerate human hearts. Sure, it can show us what good and evil is. It can give us a *knowledge* of the MORAL LAW, but it can't cause us to *love* the MORAL LAW. It can't cause us to want to *choose* the MORAL LAW. It can't cause us to *want* to do good.

We would need a whole new nature for that. We would need brand new hearts. A kind of inner spiritual regeneration. And this is where the Bible holds the answers. God tells us that this is all possible.

In this section we're going to explore how.

HOW CIVIL LAWS RELATE TO THE MORAL LAW

Firstly, we have to make this point: Remember how I said that civil laws tend to be underpinned by the MORAL LAW? How the MORAL LAW has been foundational to our constitutions and judiciary systems? You might present that idea with this sort of image:

THE MORAL LAW

Because I live in Great Britain I am subject to the civil laws of the Great Britain. And those civil laws have historically been underpinned by the MORAL LAW. The MORAL LAW says that theft is wrong so the British law that sits on top of it says that theft is illegal. The MORAL LAW says that murder is wrong so the British law that sits on top of it says that murder is illegal.

Now what if Great Britain, as a political entity, suddenly ceased to exist? That would mean the civil laws that govern this nation would cease to exist as well. It would no longer be breaking the law to steal or murder because there would no longer be any civil law to break. Law enforcement by police officers and judges would no longer be possible because there would be no civil law to enforce.

But would that make it *morally* ok to steal and murder on this island? Of course not. Because the MORAL LAW that underpins it would remain.

THE MORAL LAW

The MORAL LAW will always remain. Murder was morally wrong before the British government existed and it will be wrong even if it stops existing. Murder is wrong whether the government says it's wrong or not. Murder is wrong whether there's anybody to enforce it or not. Murder is wrong because the MORAL LAW says it's wrong and the MORAL LAW is eternal, constant and unchanging. It's is an expression of a God who is eternal, constant and unchanging. The MORAL LAW has no beginning and no end because God has no beginning and no end.

In other words, civil laws come and go and are variable, but the MORAL LAW is not.

THE LAW OF MOSES

Now when God established the nation of Israel in the Old Testament through Moses, they too needed a civil law to govern their land. And this civil law was also to be underpinned by God's character, as expressed through the eternal MORAL LAW.

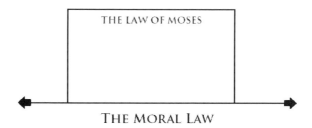

THE LAW OF MOSES

THE MORAL LAW

Back in the book of Genesis, God had promised Abraham that his descendants would become a great nation and that they would inherit a piece of land that they could call their own. This nation was Israel.

However, God's promise wasn't brought to completion straight away. Through various twists and turns of events over many generations, Abraham's descendants found themselves in slavery in Egypt. And it was while they were in slavery in Egypt that God raised up Moses to release them from that bondage so that they could inherit the land flowing with milk and honey that had been promised to Abraham years before. It was in that land that they were to form their new nation.

Most people know the story of how Moses confronted Pharaoh and how God sent plagues upon the land to force him to release His people. But perhaps what's less well known is that they didn't reach their new piece of real estate straight away. In fact, they ended up wandering in the Sinai desert for 40 years.

The period in the wilderness before they inherited the land was an important time of preparation for the people. And it was during this time that God gave Moses the civil laws that were to govern them in their new nation. Every nation needs a written constitution or legal framework and this would be theirs. Moses wrote the laws down and therefore, it has become known as the *Law of Moses* or the *Mosaic Law*.

The most well-known section of the Mosaic Law is the ten commandments, which were written in tablets of stone at the top of Mount Sinai. Pretty much everyone knows about them - even if just through the Cecil B Demille movie starring Charlton Heston - and they helped form the moral core of the law. But the whole law was actually far more extensive than just ten commandments. There were actually 613 individual rules altogether. 365 of them were negatives (you shall nots) and 248 of them were positives (you shalls).

The 613 laws could broadly be divided into three categories:

1. Moral laws (e.g. don't murder, don't steal etc.)
2. Ceremonial laws (instructions on religious observance, worship, structure of the priesthood, sacrifices etc.)
3. Social laws (how to run society, the economy, resolve disputes, care for the land etc.)

In other words this law was to govern every single aspect of life in the brand new nation of Israel. A bit like the British civil law does here. Or the Swedish law does in Sweden. Or the Canadian law does in Canada. And just as the British civil law doesn't apply in Japan or Norway or Mexico or Ghana or anywhere else, the Law of Moses didn't apply anywhere else either. It was for the people of Israel and their brand new country only.

God was in effect, the theocratic king of the nation state of Israel - at this early stage they had no human king - and as head of state, He was giving a written law for His people to live by in their new country just like a human king would have done. This law was signed off with a covenant from God which basically said that if they followed the law well, they would experience a three-fold blessing of prosperity, health and safety. However, if they disobeyed the law they would experience a three-fold curse of poverty, sickness and terror. For as long as the Law of Moses was in effect, these promises would also apply.

You can read about the promises of this covenant by opening up the Bible at Deuteronomy 28. You can also read about the laws themselves in the book of Leviticus.

The Law of Moses governed Israel's moral, religious and civil life for the rest of the Old Testament period. Right up until the death and resurrection of Jesus Christ. And when you read about 'the law' in the Bible or hear a Christian talking about 'the law', this is almost always what's being referred to - the Law of Moses.

CHAPTER 7
UNDERSTANDING THE LAW OF MOSES

Let's now go into the Law of Moses in a little more depth so that we have a fuller understanding of what it was about.

We've already noted that there were three broad types of law:

- Moral Laws
- Ceremonial Laws
- Social Laws

Let's look at each of these categories in a bit more detail.

THE MORAL PART OF THE LAW

When the people of Israel were led out of Egypt and across the Sinai desert, they had no real understanding of God. Their relationship with Him was still very new and without a real concept of God, they had no real concept of Absolute Good. They didn't have that reference point.

What's more, because they had just come out of a pagan culture in Egypt where the demonic gods behaved like humans or worse, they were used to being surrounded by immorality and had been given no real insight into holiness or righteousness by those idols.

Again, because they had not yet seen Absolute Good, they had no real understanding of what it meant to be righteous. So they had no real understanding of their own sinfulness by comparison. They didn't know the Good Apple to recognise their own mouldiness and they didn't know the Absolute Light to recognise their own darkness. The people of Israel were largely ignorant of their own sin.

The purpose of the moral part of the Law of Moses was to show them what Absolute Goodness looked like. It was designed to show them the Good Apple and to show them Absolute Light. It would explain to them that God was holier than they could ever have imagined. His moral standard, benchmark or fixed reference point was beyond anything they had ever known or even conceived of.

After showing them this standard, God declared that this was the standard they had to reach as well. He said, *"be holy because I am holy"* (Leviticus 11:44) In other words, *"Forget the standard you saw in Egypt and in the pagan cultures all around you. That was darkness compared to me. This is your standard. I am your standard. You must become like me. "*

The people had seen nothing like it. This moral revelation dramatically revealed the massive gulf that existed between God's standard of goodness and the people's standard of goodness. Isaiah vividly describes the chasm by saying that next to God's white hot holiness and stunning purity, our own 'goodness' suddenly looks like filthy rags (Is 64:6). In very much the same way that a midday sky suddenly makes a 5am sky look like darkness. It was a troubling revelation.

In fact, so high and so perfect was this new moral standard that there was simply no way a sinful human being could ever keep it. The Law of Moses didn't just reveal that man was a bit short of God's standard and needed to do better; it revealed that man was completely and utterly morally bankrupt before a God whose standards he just couldn't keep, no matter how hard he tried. Man was separated from God by an impassable chasm of sin. He was without hope.

For example, the ten commandments told them that they could never lie. And there is not a single human being who has ever gone a lifetime without lying. Everyone has lied.

The ten commandments also demanded that no one ever steal. Or dishonour their parents. Or become envious of their neighbours. These are things that humans do. We just do. All humans have lied and stolen and been envious and gone against their parents. As the Bible rightly says, *"For everyone has sinned; we all fall short of God's glorious standard."* (Rom 3:23) We just can't help it; it's part of our sinful nature inherited from Adam. That's a huge problem when God is looking for moral perfection saying, *"be holy, because I am holy."*

How could we ever hope to be as holy as God?

THE PUNISHMENT IS DEATH

What makes all this worse is that God explained to the people that if anyone broke His law the punishment was death. You see, God is *so* blazingly righteous that not a scrap or shred - not even an atom of sin - can exist unpunished. If even the smallest speck of sin remained unpunished in His universe, God would no longer be perfect himself and would no longer be God. As a perfect and holy judge, God must destroy it. As such, all sin, even the tiniest part, is set apart for destruction by God and so anyone that sins must die.

Because *we* sin, *we* must die.

People often think that a good God would never send anyone to hell but it's exactly His goodness that means He *must* send people to hell. God's goodness doesn't let you off the hook; it keeps you on the hook.

Imagine if a judge found a man guilty of a savage murder but then let him go unpunished. Would that be a good judge or a corrupt judge? It would be a corrupt judge of course. A good judge would see that justice was served. So the judge's goodness actually makes him dangerous to the criminal. And it's the same with God. His goodness and holiness means justice must be served and all sin must be destroyed. All this means that if you have sinned...and you have... He must destroy you. His goodness makes him dangerous to sinners like us.

If you've ever lied you're a liar and God has to destroy liars. If you've ever stolen you're a thief and God must destroy thieves. That illegal mp3 file you downloaded? That bit of chocolate you took from the refrigerator that belonged to someone else? Even that's enough sin to warrant your destruction.

It is terrifying holiness.

AW Tozer wrote, *"The vague and tenuous hope that God is too kind to punish the ungodly has become a deadly opiate for the consciences of millions."*

He also rightly said, *"We cannot grasp the true meaning of the divine holiness by thinking of someone or something very pure and then raising the concept to the highest degree we are capable of. God's holiness is not simply the best we know infinitely bettered. We know nothing like the divine holiness. It stands apart, unique, unapproachable, incomprehensible and unattainable. The natural man is blind to it. He may fear God's power and admire His wisdom, but His holiness he cannot even imagine."*

In fact, God's perfect holiness is so dangerous to imperfect beings like ourselves that when He was preparing to give Moses the ten commandments He warned the people to set up a perimeter around the base of the mountain and not to let anyone go past it. He told them that if any sinful human being went through the perimeter and came into contact with God's holiness as his presence rested on the mountain they would instantly die like a fly hitting an electric fly killer.

Later on a man called Uzzah unfortunately experienced the truth of this warning when he touched the Ark of the Covenant where God's presence resided by mistake - and instantly dropped dead. This kind of perfect purity was stunning to the people. It struck them with fear and awe. They had never witnessed anything like it. And God was asking them to be that perfect too?! Impossible! The people of Israel had problems...

THE CEREMONIAL PART

God actually knew the morality He was giving the people was too high for them to attain. He knew they would fall short in their efforts. And so He gave them the ceremonial part of the law. The ceremonial part of the law said, *"when you inevitably break the moral part of the law, you will defile yourself and your just punishment will be death. However I will provide a way by which you can effectively cleanse yourself of guilt and thereby make yourself right again in my sight. That way, you can go on living."* The ceremonial part of the law provided instructions on how to carry this out.

Basically, the plan was this: The people would find a pure and unblemished animal and they would take it to the temple where the priest would perform a ritual that effectively transferred the guilt of the human to the animal.

Then, with the sins of the human being effectively transferred to the animal, the priest would sacrifice the animal and the sin would be punished in its body. The animal would effectively suffer the death that belonged to the human so that the human could go free. The animal would pay the debt.

Now I know a lot of atheists like to portray God as a blood thirsty monster because of this kind of thing, but it's got to be noted that God didn't even like this system. He didn't enjoy seeing animals sacrificed at all. The writer of Hebrews tells us, *"You [God]did not want animal sacrifices or grain offerings or animals burned on the altar or other offerings for sin, nor were you pleased with them (though they are required by the Law of Moses)."* (Heb 10:8)

In Isaiah God himself says, *"I am sick of your burnt offerings of rams and the fat of fattened cattle. I get no pleasure from the blood of bulls and lambs and goats."* God says He wishes they would just be obedient to His moral law so that they didn't have to sacrifice any animals at all. He says, *"Give up your evil ways, learn to do good. Seek justice. Help the oppressed. Defend the cause of orphans. Fight for the rights of widows."* (Isaiah 1:11, 16-17)

Samuel said, *"Listen! Obedience is better than sacrifice, and submission is better than offering the fat of rams."* (1 Sam 15:22)

God would have preferred if His people were just obedient to His moral requirements so that there was never any cause to shed any blood. It brought him no pleasure to see sacrifices. But because of His goodness, His righteousness and perfection, all sin has to be punished with death and there is no other way around it. Justice demands that sin is dealt with. And God is infinitely just.

Basically, the ceremonial part of the law was just a concession to human weakness. When you play a video game, you don't want to crash the racing car or cause your character to fall off the cliff, but if you make a mistake and things go wrong, it's good to know there's a continue or reset button that allows you to keep going. It's the same thing with the ceremonial law. It wasn't God's desire to have animals killed but it acted like a continue button - a last resort for sinful people who couldn't help but go wrong and who therefore deserved to die.

The spilling of blood was also a troubling visual reminder of just how serious their sins were. It taught them never to take their sins lightly.

Now it's important to note that the ceremonial part of the law involved very specific instructions on things like circumcision, temple design, diet, clothing, tithing, rituals, sacrifices and consecrated objects. It was a lot of work to keep that system going and it was a full time job for the priests of the temple. And it meant that, using our symbol language, the Mosaic system looked like this.

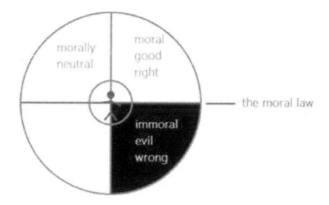

the moral law

Notice how the red line creating rights and wrongs in the moral realm (right hand side) now extends into morally neutral things as well on the left hand side. So for example, clothes are morally neutral but under the Law of Moses there were rules about clothes. Food is morally neutral but under the Law of Moses there were rules about food. Money is morally neutral but under the Law of Moses there were rules about money. The individual was expected to have a *knowledge* of these things and was expected to *obey* them too.

Now why would God do this? Why would he create rules on what people could eat and drink and wear? Why would he be so arbitrary?

Well, the laws weren't actually that arbitrary at all. In fact, often they were for the people's own health and protection.

For example, God told them not to eat shellfish. Now we might think that's a little harsh but even today, when someone is struck down with food poisoning, the culprit is more often than not those slightly whiffy clams from the buffet. Shellfish is notorious for absorbing the pollution of its environment and causing sickness in anyone who eats them.

In the same way, God took mushrooms off the menu for Israel. Mushrooms can be highly poisonous, are difficult to tell apart, and will easily kill.

God said to make sure meat was fully cooked and blood was drained properly. Again, we know that blood infections are often fatal, even today.

God said not to eat pork. Do a little research on the facts about pig meat and you'll discover this was particularly good advice, especially in those days.

So God was actually protecting the health of His people with these rules.

THE SOCIAL PART

Finally, the third category of law was the social or civil part. Like our own civil laws, these set the boundaries of how people were to interact with one another, resolve disputes and generally create a stable and harmonious society. If the ceremonial part of the law kept people right with God then the social part of the law kept people right with each other.

The social part of the law also involved instructions on neutral things. For example it stated that every seven years all debts should be reset. It said that every seven years the farm land should be rested so that it remained productive with food.

And actually, if you'll allow me to go off on a slight tangent here, one of the accusations often levelled at the Bible is that it the Law of Moses appears to condone slavery. The truth is that while it's true that people could put themselves into slavery to pay off a debt to another, the social part of the law insisted that all debts had to be cancelled and slaves had to be freed every seventh year. So this wasn't slavery in the way that we think of it today. It's a bit like when you can't pay a restaurant bill so you spend the evening washing dishes for free to pay off the debt. People could put themselves under the ownership of another doing unpaid work to pay off a debt, but the owner was commanded by law to release that person back into freedom within 7 years. (Deut 15:1, Jer 34:14)

So each part of the law interacted. The moral part was designed to reveal how morally bankrupt the people were in the eyes of God and then the idea was that they would then be driven towards the ceremonial part with its rituals to atone for their sin. The shedding of blood would be a potent reminder of the severity of their wrong-doing before a holy God. And then the social part of the law would keep people right with one another and maintain a stable and harmonious society.

ONE LAW

But even though I've just been talking about the Law of Moses as though it had three distinct parts, and although it's common for teachers to divide it like that for the purpose of analysis, it's important to realise that the Law of Moses is actually a single and indivisible unit. All 613 rules functioned as one. And I can't stress that enough.

Today it's extremely common for people to try to separate the ten commandments from the other 603 rules but we simply can't do that. In fact, the term, *Ten Commandments* doesn't even exist in the Bible. The whole LAW OF MOSES is simply known collectively as "The Law". In Basic Theology, Charles C Rhynie states:

"...the Jewish people either did not acknowledge [the three-fold division] or at least did not insist on it. Rather they divided the 613 commandments of the Law into twelve families of commandments which were then subdivided into twelve additional families of positive and twelve additional families of negative commands."

Because there is no division between the types of laws, they actually sit side-by-side and run on from one another in the Bible. For example in Leviticus 19:18 we read, *"do not bear a grudge or seek revenge"* which is a moral command. But then in the very next verse (v19) we read, *"do not plant your field with two different kinds of seed"*, which is a social law. There's no obvious distinction or separation between the two types of law in the text. It was a complete unit.

BREAKING THE LAW

What this meant was that if someone broke just one of the 613 rules that made up the law, they broke the whole unit.

In other words, if they kept 612 of the rules but broke the 613th, they were guilty of breaking the whole thing. And it didn't matter which 'category' of law they broke because it all functioned as one.

We do that today as well. Take our civil law not to murder. That's a moral law. And then take our civil law not to break the speed limit. That's not a moral law; it's a social one. It's not any more immoral to drive at 61mph than it is at 60mph. But whether someone murders or breaks the speed limit we use the same expression - we say that they have broken *the* law. Singular. The same civil authority has been offended by each transgression. And it's the same with the Law of Moses.

Whichever one of the 613 laws you broke, whether it be moral, ceremonial or social, it was an offence to the same authority - God. And because of His holiness, God punishes all sin the same way - by death.

Now imagine if someone was caught breaking the speed limit and then pleaded their case in front of a human judge by saying, *'well yes, I was speeding...but I haven't murdered anyone... so I think you should let me go without a punishment.'* The judge would say, *'it's good you haven't murdered anyone but you have still broken the law and therefore, I have to punish you for the crime you have committed.'* In other words, keeping all the other laws doesn't make you immune from punishment for the one you have broken. You can't atone for wrong-doing by keeping the rest. If you break one, whichever it is, you deserve punishment for it.

In the same way, the people of Israel couldn't say to God, "Yes, I've broken 1 law but I've kept the other 612 so I don't deserve punishment." God would say, "it's good you've kept 612 but I still have to punish you for the 1 that you have broken. You have still sinned."

And under the Law of Moses the punishment for all sin was death.

What I'm trying to communicate here is that if there is a law, the only way to fully satisfy it is to keep it perfectly and if you don't satisfy it to the last detail, you are deserving of punishment. For Israel, all transgression of the law meant death so even keeping 612 of the laws and breaking just 1 would mean death because of the righteousness of God.

This means that someone who only broke some of the laws was actually in no better shape than someone who broke them all. They would both be under the same curse of death. They would both be headed for the same punishment. The Bible says, *"Cursed is anyone who does not affirm and obey the terms of these instructions"* (Deut 27:26). So if we can be stark about it, the Law of Moses actually put *everyone* under a curse of death because literally not a single person could keep all the 613 rules perfectly.

This was the real point of the Law of Moses then - to show the people that they fell short of God's perfect moral standard and that without the sacrificial shedding of blood for their sins by another on their behalf, they themselves would die.

CHAPTER 8
THE HEART CAN BE CURED

At first, life in this new nation under the Law of Moses went reasonably well. They generally adhered to the law and when they made mistakes they humbly went to God with their sacrifice to be ceremonially cleansed. Because they were trying to obey the law, their nation experienced the blessing of prosperity, health and safety that had been promised to them under the covenant with God and an early pinnacle was reached under the righteous rulership of King David.

Unfortunately, things were never quite that good again.

From glorious heights of David's reign they plunged into a decline, turning from God to follow pagan idols. By abandoning their moral reference point, their moral compasses broke, immorality soon followed and evil began to spread throughout the land. Though God was patient with them and gave them warnings ahead of time to return to him, their behaviour didn't improve and the curses of the covenant began to come into play. Instead of prosperity, health and safety, Israel began experiencing poverty, sickness and terror. Foreign nations invaded and destroyed their city walls, scattering the people from their homes. Sickness and disease ravaged the land and depression and despair gripped the hearts of the people. Eventually they ended up in bondage.

When we consider that God had told them up front that obedience would lead to blessing and disobedience would lead to curses for their nation it seems like insanity that they would choose to be disobedient anyway. Who would deliberately choose curses over blessing? If you have two paths before you - one leading to blessing and the other curses - why would you choose the one that leads to the curse? But you'll remember that our inherent heart corruption means we just can't help it. Moral entropy will always take hold.

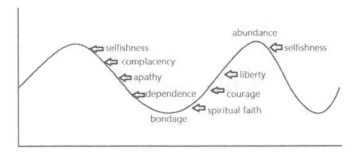

As Tytler observed from history, when God blesses the people with abundance they begin to think they achieved the blessing by their own efforts and that they don't need God anymore, they turn away from him towards selfishness, and the whole thing starts to fall apart. Poverty, sickness and terror...and eventually bondage, inevitably follows. Israel's experience highlights this phenomenon perfectly and confirms the entropy at work within the human heart. It naturally leans *away* from God towards selfishness and self-interest - ***even when we know things will end badly by our actions.***

Jeremiah wrote, *"The heart is more deceitful than all else and desperately sick; who can understand it?"* (Jer 17:9) We don't even understand it ourselves.

Who can understand why a married man gives up his wife and family for one selfish night of adultery? Often he doesn't even understand his own actions and regrets it for the rest of his life. How many people wake up with a terrible hangover in a morning and ask themselves why they drank so much the previous night? How many people hurt someone else and then afterwards ask themselves why they lashed out? How many people have regrets because they inexplicably did something that they knew was wrong? We often can't understand our own behaviour. Often, we know ahead of time that things are going to end badly if we take a certain path and yet we do it anyway.

Paul explains this frustrating phenomenon when he says: *"I want to do what is right, but I can't. I want to do what is good, but I don't. I don't want to do what is wrong, but I do it anyway. But if I do what I don't want to do, I am not really the one doing wrong; it is sin living in me that does it." (Rom 7:18-20)*

The sin living within us. That's the key. The only reason we ever sin is because in that moment, our heart wants to. It's that simple. We know it's wrong; we know it's going to end badly; we know we're taking the wrong path; but the strength of desire for sin in our hearts can be so strong - we want to indulge it *so* much - that it overrides our conscience, our knowledge of right and wrong - and we go ahead and do it anyway. That's the terminal sickness that we have in our hearts. That's the inherent corruption we carry that causes us to do things we don't even want to do. And it's this inherent corruption that meant the Law of Moses was always going to be abandoned. It was completely inevitable that Israel would eventually turn away from it, and God, towards self-interest.

And we can't criticise them because we would have been just the same.

The Law of Moses was good but like any law, it had no power to overcome this heart sickness. It had no power to stop people from loving their sin. It could show people a midday sky but it couldn't stop them from preferring the darkness. It could show people what a Good Apple looks like but it couldn't stop them from loving their own rotten cores. It could show people what sin looks like but it couldn't stop them from loving their sin. In the same way that laws wouldn't stop me from loving chocolate and prohibition didn't stop people from loving alcohol, the law had no power to change their desires.

The law never imparts righteousness. It doesn't change what our hearts want.

Despite being given the Law of Moses, Israel still had no inclination to go after goodness. And they never *would* have any inclination under that system.

God described their heart sickness saying, *"Your injury is incurable - a terrible wound. There is no one to plead your cause or to bind up your injury. No medicine can heal you."* (Jer 30:12-13)

They were in a bit of a hopeless situation. Without internal renovation; without new hearts; they were doomed to eternally keep breaking God's laws, becoming slaves to self in the process, and ultimately bringing themselves and their country to ruin, bondage and death. Life under the LAW OF MOSES was not going well and it seemed like there was no solution.

THE SOLUTION

It *seemed* like there was no solution...but there was. God had the solution.

In the midst of this hopelessness, while Israel was at its lowest ebb and the nation lay in ruins because of the sin of the people, God started to make some very exciting promises:

"And I will give you a new heart, and I will put a new spirit in you. I will take out your stony, stubborn heart and give you a tender, responsive heart. And I will put my Spirit in you so that you will follow my decrees and be careful to obey my regulations." (Eze 36:26-27)

You'll understand how exciting this promise was. Here God was promising a cure for humanity's heart corruption! He was talking about a way to give people new hearts! This could potentially change everything....

Through Ezekiel, God said that a time was coming when they would not only *know* what Absolute Good was but that they'd *crave* it. They would want to *choose* it. He would do this by putting His own Spirit inside His people and transforming their hearts. With promises of internal renovation, suddenly there was hope for the people of Israel and ultimately the whole of mankind.

"The day is coming," says the LORD, "when I will make a new covenant with the people of Israel and Judah. This covenant will not be like the one I made with their ancestors when I took them by the hand and brought them out of the land of Egypt. They broke that covenant, though I loved them as a husband loves his wife," says the LORD.

"But this is the new covenant I will make with the people of Israel on that day," says the LORD. "I will put my instructions deep within them, and I will write them on their hearts. I will be their God, and they will be my people. (Jer 31:31-33)

Instead of writing His laws on external parchment and tablets of stone as He had done at Sinai, He was instead going to write His instructions deep within the hearts of His people and heal them internally. He goes further in explaining how this would happen saying:

"The day will come when I will do for Israel and Judah all the good things I have promised them. In those days and at that time I will raise up a righteous descendant from King David's line. He will do what is just and right throughout the land...And this will be his name: 'the LORD is our righteousness.'" (Jer 33:15-16)

"The LORD is our righteousness." Remember that vital phrase. Remember how God had told Israel that they needed to *"be holy because I am holy"* and we wondered how that could ever be possible? We wondered how anyone could ever be considered as holy as God. But here God appears to be saying that a Messiah would come along who would create a way to make that possible. Somehow people would be able to claim the required perfect, godly righteousness through him. Wow.

God was even more specific about this Messiah. He said he would come through the royal lineage of King David, he would introduce a brand new covenant, a new relationship between men and God, and a new dispensation of time. He would change everything.

The Messiah was Jesus Christ. And for hundreds of years prior to His birth the people of Israel waited for him knowing that He was their only hope of salvation from bondage, sin and death.

THE RISE OF THE PHARISEES

Now here's where it gets a little complicated. Because in the 400 years before Jesus, the Messiah, arrived to fulfil the prophecy of this new covenant, a group of strict religious Jews called the Pharisees came along to muddy the waters.

The Pharisees understood that Israel had fallen into ruins primarily because the people had turned their back on God and brought poverty, sickness and terror upon themselves by their own sinful disobedience. And they had spotted that it was the people's own licentious living, sexual immorality, drunkenness and idol worship that had ruined the land. They were determined that was never going to happen again and they weren't going to sit around waiting for a Messiah either. They were going to fix this problem themselves.

Their solution? Their man-made solution?

More laws. Stricter laws. Harsher laws.

Now as we know already, you can't make people good by law. Whether there is 1 law against eating chocolate, 10 laws against eating chocolate or 100 laws against eating chocolate, I'm still going to want to eat chocolate. Increasing the number of laws doesn't affect my desire for it. And likewise, if we have a desire to sin within our hearts, it doesn't matter how many laws there are against it, we're still going to want to do it.

In fact, giving more laws to a person with an unregenerate heart is just giving them more laws to break.

So this man-made solution was always doomed to failure.

But here was the thinking: if the people hadn't behaved under 613 rules, then they would behave under 800. And should people break these 800 laws, or twist or bend them, or find loopholes to exploit, the Pharisees would solve that problem by introducing even more laws to tighten the loop holes and make it even more rigid. And if need be, more laws on top of those. And so on.

Eventually, with enough laws in place, people would be so restricted and coerced by rules, that they would be *forced* to act in the right way. They would have no other option. And at that point, a good society would emerge that God would approve of.

Indeed, the thinking was that they would gain some kind of extra credit with God for going above and beyond the obligations of the original 613 laws. The more laws they kept to prove their devotion to him, the more strict they were with themselves, the more He would love them. So they turned the law into a system of merit. Keep more laws; be more loved.

Over time the Pharisees actually added hundreds of man-made laws to the original written Law of Moses and these man-made rules became known as the *Oral Law*.

THIS IS LEGALISM

This is legalism. Trying to regulate behaviour through law.

To give an example of how their plan developed, the written Law of Moses had originally said not to do any work on the Sabbath. That was the fourth of the ten commandments. For most people that meant taking a break from their every-day job to rest and recuperate. God gave that law because he knew that if people worked seven days a week they would burn out and it wouldn't be good for their health. He told them to take a day off for their own benefit.

But then the Pharisees came along and said, *"It's not enough just to take a day off work. To be super dedicated to God, to make God really love you the most, you should not even lift anything burdensome on the Sabbath. Because just lifting something burdensome technically counts as work!"*

And then that threw up another question: *"what constitutes 'something burdensome'?"* Could they lift up their child? Was that too heavy? Could they lift up a leaf? Did that count as work?

So they needed more laws to define the new laws. They defined the weight of a 'burden' as *"food in weight equal to a dried fig, wine enough for a mixing goblet, milk enough for one swallow, ink enough to write two letters of the alphabet."*

But then that raises more questions...

Like how big can the mixing goblet be? Is there a standardised measurement? And what constitutes a 'swallow' of milk? Surely some people take bigger gulps than others? And so on and so on. Rules begets rules begets rules. A constant effort to tighten up loopholes so that people are forced to act in 'the right way'.

You can see how ridiculous and arbitrary this became. All of a sudden people were refusing to carry two glasses of milk on the Sabbath because it was illegal according to the Oral Law. They wouldn't lift up their child to give them a cuddle in case others saw them and their Sabbath breaking caused a scandal. Someone was considered cut off from God because they'd lifted a handful of dried figs. It's almost laughable but this became religion to the Jews. A swamp of petty rules and regulations with sub rules and sub sub rules and sub sub sub rules, until there were so many rules they were submerged under their oppressive weight. Again, we call this kind of religion, *legalism*. Legalism is trying to get right with God using law or rule-keeping and trying to use laws to regulate behaviour. Using our language of symbols, the Pharisees did something like this:

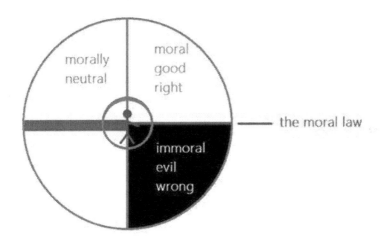

They really thickened up that left hand bar by creating a myriad of new rules on neutral issues to try to restrict, coerce and control the people. What you could lift, wear, eat, at different times, on different days. Paul wrote about this kind of legalism saying, *"These rules may seem wise because they require strong devotion, pious self-denial, and severe bodily discipline. But they provide no help in conquering a person's evil desires."*(Col 2:23) Again, law doesn't impart righteousness. The heart sickness still remained. The sinful nature remained unconquered.

In fact, burdening unregenerate hearts with excessive laws creates a whole new raft of problems. It had disastrous consequences.

THE PROBLEMS WITH LEGALISM

Firstly, it made the people hard-hearted in the name of religion. People would refuse to cuddle their child on the Sabbath because lifting them up would be deemed as breaking the rules. It meant that if there was an injured person on the street you couldn't show hospitality towards them on the Sabbath because helping them would be seen as work. The Bible records Jesus and His disciples walking through a field of grain around lunchtime on the Sabbath and being hungry, they began eating some of the grain as they went. The Pharisees saw this and were furious, calling it harvesting. They would have rather people went hungry than broke their petty rules. This is the cold and loveless behaviour that legalism promotes.

And then secondly, there was pride. Legalism drove them into competition with one another. One man would see another lifting a jug of milk on the Sabbath and feel superior because he hadn't broken that particular law. His pride would tell him to disassociate with this sinner who obviously didn't have the same kind of righteous devotion as he. Love, kindness and mercy became distance concepts to the Pharisees.

"You keep 602 laws do you? Well I keep 608! God must love me more!"

" You lift up a milk jug on the Sabbath do you? I won't even lift up a glass! That's how pious I am!"

The Pharisees looked down on anyone who didn't keep the rules as well as they did because they perceived such people to be further down the table of merit. They had no time for sinners either. They had no time for prostitutes, beggars or any of the other lowly members of society. They saw such people as being unworthy of them.

They also began competing to make public shows of their good deeds, just to make sure everyone else could see how pious and loved by God they were. When they fasted they made sure everyone knew about it. They would go out in public deliberately looking dishevelled and sick to emphasise their lack of sustenance and therefore, their piety. When they gave donations to charity they made sure everyone knew how much they were giving. Such things became a method of gaining esteem in the community. And so they became more worried about what men thought of them than God. All of this behaviour was fuelled by their pride.

And the third problem with legalism is just that it completely oppressed the people. Jesus said, *"what sorrow also awaits you experts in religious law! For you crush people with unbearable religious demands, and you never lift a finger to ease the burden."* (Luke 11:46) The weight of all the laws crushed the people.

The Pharisees had completely lost sight of what the Law of Moses had been for. The law had been designed to show Israel that *everyone* has sinned and *everyone* has fallen short of God's perfect standard and that *no-one* can reach holiness by their own efforts and so *everyone* deserves death. Turning it into a system of merit to gain favour with God had missed the point entirely.

The truth is that though a Pharisee kept 612 of the laws and the prostitutes and beggars kept none, they were all still in the exact same boat. All were under the curse of death. All completely cut off from God. None of them were in a position to boast. The Pharisees were no better off.

The only way to satisfy the law is to keep it perfectly and no one could actually do that. Not even the Pharisees. They had missed the point of the law completely. Here they thought their good deeds were making them acceptable before God on a table of merit when in fact God was so stunningly holy and so perfect that their best good deeds were like filthy rags compared to His righteousness.

But finally, perhaps the biggest problem with legalism is that it inevitably leads to hypocrisy.

You see, the legalist's pride demands that they maintain an outward show of superior discipline and good deeds but their inner sinful nature - their heart sickness - remains unconquered. This means they are physically incapable of keeping the increasing mountain of burdensome rules that they are imposing upon themselves. So the gap between who they claim to be on the outside and who they really are on the inside begins to widen. They are under increasing pressure to hide their true selves from the world and it becomes a burden to them. They do anything to sustain the facade, to protect their public image, to cover up their sin from the eyes of the world, to keep their pride and social standing in tact, but inside they are completely unchanged. For this reason, the Pharisees gradually became all show and no substance.

JESUS CLASHES WITH THE PHARISEES

It should be noted that the biggest opposition to Jesus Christ as the Messiah didn't come from lowly sinners; it came from these Pharisees. The legalists. The ones who thought they had more religion than anyone. And it was the Pharisees for whom Jesus reserved His harshest words of criticism. In fact, He frequently referred to them as hypocrites and even called them sons of hell (Matt 23:15). He called them whitewashed tombs which looked nice on the outside but inside were full of decay and impurity. He also likened them to unwashed cups which looked clean on the outside but inside were full of dirt, greed, and self indulgence. Jesus didn't hold back with these guys.

Paul wrote about them saying, *"You are so proud of knowing the law but you dishonour God by breaking it...The world blasphemes the name of God because of you."* (Rom 2:23-24) Paul acknowledged that where non-Christians see this kind of hypocritical, cold, legalistic religion with no substance, no love and no humility, it turns people away from God.

I have friends who were brought up under the oppressive weight of heavy legalism in a group called The Brethren. They were banned from doing anything on a Sunday. No sport, no activity of any kind, not even washing the dirty dishes. They had to wear suits for the entire day. Anything else was considered sinful. At Christmas their parents would go to religious conferences to keep up appearances instead of spending time with their children. TVs and video games weren't allowed in the house. The hypocrisy of that was that when they wanted to watch something, they would just go to someone else's house and watch it there instead. All this meant they could make an outward show of piety to their religious visitors by pointing out that they didn't have a TV, but all the while they were just popping out to watch their shows elsewhere when it suited them.

A kind of comical charade developed where everyone in the church knew about each other's hypocrisy but no one would say a word about it because they were secretly doing the exact same thing. The bubble of illusion that pride had created couldn't be punctured. When, eventually, my friend's parents caved in and bought a TV of their own and allowed video games, they still hid it out of sight to keep the illusion going.

As I said, this hypocrisy was going on amongst the entire congregation.

Furthermore, many of them worked as fishermen and whilst at home they would keep the mask of piety on for the community, as soon as they went to sea they would indulge in smoking, drinking and swearing. As soon as they felt free of having to maintain a social facade, their real, inner, unchanged, selves came to the fore. They were hypocrites, whitewashed tombs, unwashed cups. And it was that harsh, hard-hearted legalism and prideful hypocrisy that turned those friends off God. Paul's words are true - the world blasphemes God because of such hypocritical legalism.

Jesus said of the Pharisees, *"The teachers of religious law and the Pharisees...crush you with impossible religious demands and never lift a finger to help ease the burden. Everything they do is for show. On their arms they wear extra wide prayer boxes with scripture verses inside and they wear extra long tassels on their robes. And how they love to sit at the head table in banquets and in the most prominent seats in the* synagogue! *They enjoy the attention they get on the streets and they enjoy being called Rabbi...How terrible it will be for you teachers of religious law and the Pharisees. Hypocrites!"* (Matt 23:2, 4-7, 13)

Again, you have to understand that these people thought that God loved them the most! They prided themselves in the fact they knew more about the law than anyone. And they prided themselves that they kept all these extra man-made rules. So imagine how shocked they were and infuriated when Jesus came along saying, *"their worship is a farce, and they teach man-made ideas as commands from God."* (Matt 15:9) and then went on to tell them that they were actually the furthest from God, that they were sons of hell and the worst of all hypocrites!

Legalists, to this very day, are exactly the same. They teach man-made ideas as though they are commands from God and imagine that He must love them the most because they keep the most rules. But always remember that Jesus was opposed most fiercely by, and reserved His harshest words for, legalists - not for sinners.

CHAPTER 9
THE MESSIAH ARRIVES

So before the Pharisees came along to mangle the Law of Moses, it's original design was to teach Israel one basic principle - that all people fall short of God's perfect standard and that all sin must be punished with death before a holy God. It was really that simple. If you have sinned...and you have...you deserve death. And either you pay that debt of death yourself or you can transfer your guilt to an innocent creature and sacrifice it on your behalf. But there can be no forgiveness of sin without the shedding of blood (Heb 9:22).

What they didn't realise was that through this sacrificial system, God was giving them an exact picture of what the Messiah was going to do for them.

The law was a foreshadow of the Messiah.

You see, Jesus Christ was going to come into the world, live a perfectly pure and unblemished life, fulfilling the moral and social requirements of the law perfectly, and then, having done so, just like those blameless sacrificial lambs under the old covenant, He would willingly take the sin of the world upon himself so that the ceremonial punishment of death that we deserve could be carried out in His own body. He was going to be God's own sacrifice for our sin. God's own sacrificial Lamb.

He would be put to death by crucifixion taking *our* guilt upon himself so that *we* could be forgiven and go on living. He would become our eternal 'continue' button. His death would mean we could go on living forever.

All those exciting prophecies about a Messiah from King David's lineage were about to come true. And although we only looked at a few of those prophecies in the previous chapter, there were actually over 300 of them scattered throughout the Old Testament. God repeatedly told His prophets that this was going to happen. And when Jesus arrived, he fulfilled all those prophecies perfectly.

This is, in fact, one of the ways that we know the Bible is divinely inspired.

Mathematician Peter Stoner calculated that the chance of one man fulfilling just eight of the prophecies about Jesus accidentally was 1 in 10^{17} which, when written out fully, is 1 in 100,000,000,000,000,000. Stoner further calculated that one man fulfilling just 48 of the Old Testament prophecies about Jesus by chance would be 1 in $10^{157.}$ When we start considering how one person could fulfil *hundreds* of prophecies by chance, we get into figures that are impossible to comprehend. The maths alone tells us the Messiah's arrival was by divine appointment.

One of the most famous prophecies of what Jesus was going to do was given to Isaiah who wrote the following passage a full 700 years before Jesus arrived:

"There was nothing beautiful or majestic about his appearance,
nothing to attract us to him.
He was despised and rejected—
a man of sorrows, acquainted with deepest grief.
We turned our backs on him and looked the other way.
He was despised, and we did not care.

Yet it was our weaknesses he carried;
*   it was our sorrows that weighed him down.*
* And we thought his troubles were a punishment from God,*
*   a punishment for his own sins!*
But he was pierced for our rebellion,
*   crushed for our sins.*
* He was beaten so we could be whole.*
*   He was whipped so we could be healed.*
All of us, like sheep, have strayed away.
*   We have left God's paths to follow our own.*
* Yet the LORD laid on him*
*   the sins of us all.*

He was oppressed and treated harshly,
*   yet he never said a word.*
* He was led like a lamb to the slaughter.*
*   And as a sheep is silent before the shearers,*
*   he did not open his mouth.*
Unjustly condemned,
*   he was led away.*
* No one cared that he died without descendants,*
*   that his life was cut short in midstream.*
* But he was struck down*
*   for the rebellion of my people.*
He had done no wrong
*   and had never deceived anyone.*
* But he was buried like a criminal;*
*   he was put in a rich man's grave.*

But it was the LORD's good plan to crush him
*   and cause him grief.*
* Yet when his life is made an offering for sin,*

he will have many descendants.
He will enjoy a long life,
and the LORD's good plan will prosper in his hands.
When he sees all that is accomplished by his anguish,
he will be satisfied.
And because of his experience,
my righteous servant will make it possible
for many to be counted righteous,
for he will bear all their sins.
I will give him the honours of a victorious soldier,
because he exposed himself to death.
He was counted among the rebels.
He bore the sins of many and interceded for rebels.

Isaiah 53

This prophecy told people that Jesus was to be pierced for *our* rebellion and crushed for *our* sin. God was to lay on *him* the sins of *us* all. The Bible says, *"For God made Christ, who never sinned, to be the offering for our sin, so that we could be made right with God through Christ."* (2 Cor 5:21)

This is the stunning core of the gospel. That God loved the *whole* world so much that He gave His one and only begotten Son, so that *everyone* who believes in him will not perish but have eternal life. (John 3:16) And unlike the Old Testament sacrificial system where one person would bring one sacrificial lamb to bear His own sin, Jesus - God's sacrificial Lamb - had the sin of the *whole* world laid upon him. This created a way for anyone to claim freedom from death through that one sacrifice. Paul says, *"Christ has rescued us from the curse [of death] pronounced by the law. When he was hung on the cross, he took upon himself the curse for our wrongdoing."* (Gal 3:13)

As astonishing as it is that Jesus, the Son of God, would freely sacrifice himself for us like that, things would get even more astonishing still.

Because when lambs were sacrificed under the Law of Moses they generally stayed dead. The Lamb of God however...would not. Having laid down His life to pay the debt for our sin, on the third day Jesus rose again from the grave, conquering death in the process, and in His triumph, He won the power to raise us from the dead too (Rev 1:18). As Jesus himself put it, *"Because I live, you also will live"*. (John 14:19) and *"I am the resurrection and the life. Anyone who believes in me will live, even after dying. Everyone who lives in me and believes in me will never ever die."* (John 11:25-26)

This is why Paul triumphantly exclaims, *"Death is swallowed up in victory. O death, where is your victory? O death, where is your sting? For sin is the sting that results in death, and the law gives sin its power. But thank God! He gives us victory over sin and death through our Lord Jesus Christ!"* (1 Cor 15:55-57)

The cross of Christ is the pivotal event in world history.

WHERE LOVE AND JUSTICE MEET

An innocent man, even God in human flesh, sacrifices himself to save His creation. Has there ever been a more loving act than that? Can we even comprehend that kind of love? In the same way the Israelites were stunned by God's perfect holiness when they were led out of Egypt, we should be equally stunned by the love that led him to die for us. And it's in the cross that those two elements of God's character are clearly seen. Both His love and His holiness.

The picture of the cross vividly tells us that God is so holy that He must punish sin with death. We've talked a lot about that aspect of God's character so far and that never changes. But the cross also tells us that God is so loving that He preferred to take the punishment that we deserve upon himself rather than let us suffer.

Here's a parable that might explain it.

There were once a pair of best friends who grew up together. They were extremely close and regarded each other as brothers. At college one studied law and the other studied business. After graduation the one who had studied law became a judge in his hometown while the other had to leave to seek employment. Because of the distance between them they gradually fell out of touch and lost contact. The judge tried to contact his friend on several occasions but to no avail. One day, many years later, the judge was presiding over a series of cases when he looked down at his papers to discover that the next case involved a crime so serious that it carried the death penalty. Handing out the death penalty was a grave task at the best of times, but when he looked up he was shocked and sickened to see that the defendant was in fact, his estranged childhood friend who he hadn't seen for years! He had fallen on hard times and become embroiled in serious criminal activity. What was worse was that there was no doubt that he was guilty of the crime. There were many witnesses to what he'd done and he admitted it with his own lips. He had no defence. Justice demanded that he be put to death in accordance with the law.

So this was the judge's dilemma...

If he didn't convict his friend of the crime then the law wouldn't be upheld, justice wouldn't be served and he would be a corrupt judge. That wasn't an option. However, if he *did* convict his friend, he'd be sentencing someone he loved to death. He couldn't put someone he loved to death. So that wasn't an option either. How could he be just *and* loving at the same time?

Well this is what he did...

He found his friend guilty of the crimes and handed out the death sentence. Justice demanded that he do that. And in passing the correct sentence, justice would be served. However, rather than let his friend take the punishment for his own crime, the judge himself took off his robes, came down from his lofty position of power and walked over to his friend saying, *"I can't let you take this punishment yourself. So I am going to offer myself to the executioner to pay your debt. Let my life be a substitution for yours and in my death I will purchase your freedom. Use that freedom well. You now have a second chance at life. Go home and break the law no more."* The judge then went to the executioner and gave up his life. With the demands of the law met, the friend could now go free. Justice and love would meet in that one act.

As we read that parable we should feel a little bit uneasy, if not outraged at how unfair it was that the innocent judge should sacrifice himself to let the guilty scumbag walked free. He should have died for his own crime, right? Yet this is a picture of what Jesus did for us on the cross. We were guilty. We're the scumbag in this story. He was innocent. Yet He died for us to pay our debt so we could go free. That's the beautiful scandal of grace. Jesus died so that we could go on living. He bought our freedom with his life.

"When we were utterly helpless, Christ came at just the right time and died for us sinners. Now, most people would not be willing to die for an upright person, though someone might perhaps be willing to die for a person who is especially good. But God showed his great love for us by sending Christ to die for us while we were still sinners. And since we have been made right in God's sight by the blood of Christ, he will certainly save us from God's condemnation. For since our friendship with God was restored by the death of his Son while we were still his enemies, we will certainly be saved through the life of his Son. So now we can rejoice in our wonderful new relationship with God because our Lord Jesus Christ has made us friends of God." (Rom 5:6-11)

Now all this leaves us each with a decision to make.

Because if you have lied or stolen or blasphemed His name or done anything wrong at all in your lifetime, you have broken the MORAL LAW and have a debt of death to pay. There is no use hoping that God will not punish your wrong-doing; God is a righteous judge who has to see that justice is served. He will pass the sentence of death on anyone who has sinned. He must because He is good.

The decision you're left with is whether to let God punish you for your own sin, or to humbly accept the sacrifice Jesus has already made on your behalf. Those are the only two options available to you. Either you pay your own debt of death or you accept Jesus' death in your place. There is no third option.

A Christian is simply someone who has accepted that they need a Saviour and put their faith in Jesus for eternal life. That's why we sing:

Because the sinless Saviour died
My sinful soul is counted free
For God the Just is satisfied
To look on Him and pardon me

God looks on what *He's* done and pardons me. There's nothing we can do to make ourselves right with God. We can't earn our way into heaven. Despite what the Pharisees thought, His moral standard is too high and we just keep breaking it. We have a heart sickness. Our only hope of salvation lies in what our Saviour, Jesus, has done for us. As the prophets foretold, *He* is our claim to righteousness. Our hope is in him alone. And He is the only Saviour there is because He's the only one who died to pay our debt. *"There is salvation in no one else! God has given no other name under heaven by which we must be saved."* (Acts 4:12) And Jesus was right when He said, *"I am the way, the truth and the life. No one can come to the Father (God) except through me."* (John 14:6) If you have any intention of avoiding death and hell when you stand before God on judgement day, you *need* Jesus. If you trust in any other name, whether it be Buddha, Allah, Muhammad, Vishnu, Kali, or just yourself and your own good deeds, you are without hope. Your good deeds can't atone for sin and those pagan gods are merely demons whose intentions are to draw you away from the truth. (1 Cor 10:19-20)

Paul writes in the book of Romans:

"...now God has shown us a different way of being made right in his sight – not by obeying the law but by the way promised in the scriptures long ago. We are made right in God's sight when we trust in Jesus Christ to take away our sins. And we can all be saved in this way, no matter who we are or what we have done.

For all have sinned; all fall short of God's glorious standard. Yet now God in his gracious kindness declares us not guilty. He has done this through Christ Jesus who has freed us by taking away our sins. For God sent Jesus to take the punishment for our sins and to satisfy God's anger against us. We are made right with God when we believe that Jesus shed his blood, sacrificing his life for us." – Romans 3:22-25

It doesn't matter what you have done - Jesus will save you if you'll let him. All He asks is that you repent of your sin, make him Lord of your life and put your faith in him for salvation. God has given you an escape route from the death you deserve at great personal expense - please take it. I know your pride is going to fight this. It's going to tell you that God couldn't possibly turn you away. You help old ladies across the street. You're a good person in your own eyes. I promise you that it's not enough in God's. The more you see of his light, the more you'll recognise your own darkness. And *"The soul that sins will die."* (Eze 18:20)

If you haven't done it already, humble yourself today and accept your need of a Saviour. Jesus is your *only* hope.

CHAPTER 10
THE LAW OF MOSES BECOMES OBSOLETE

Now here's where things get controversial...at least for some. Because Jesus Christ actually made the Law of Moses obsolete.

He did this by fulfilling the purpose for which the law was given.

1. He fulfilled the moral part of the law by living a perfect and holy life.
2. He fulfilled the ceremonial part of the law by dying as a sacrificial Lamb in our place.
3. He fulfilled the social part of the law by never sinning against another person.

Jesus fulfilled *every* part of the Law of Moses. All 613 rules. Perfectly.

For that reason Paul writes:

"Christ has already accomplished the purpose for which the law was given. As a result, all who believe in him are made right with God." – Romans 10:4

"The law of Moses was unable to save us because of the weakness of our sinful nature. So God did what the law could not do. He sent his own Son in a body like the bodies we sinners have. And in that body God declared an end to sin's control over us by giving his Son as a sacrifice for our sins. He did this so that

the just requirement of the law would be fully satisfied for us..."
– Romans 8:3-4

Paul is saying that Jesus did what we couldn't do. He fulfilled, accomplished or fully satisfied the Law of Moses on our behalf. We couldn't keep all those 613 rules, but He could. And because He fulfilled all of it on our behalf, that means there's nothing left for us to do but put our faith in Him and his finished work.

Think of it like this:

Imagine God's requirement for eternal life was to complete an impossible 613 piece jigsaw puzzle. He gives us this puzzle and says *'do this and you'll have eternal life'*. But we can't. It's beyond our capabilities. No matter how hard we try there is never any chance we will ever manage to complete the puzzle perfectly. So we are without hope - we have been given an impossible task.

Then imagine Jesus comes along and He *can* do it. So He sits down and puts the pieces together for us and when it's done He takes it to God and says *"I finished this on behalf of <insert your name here>."* Because Jesus has already done it for us, there's literally nothing else we can do. There's nothing we can add. There's no credit we can claim. It was all Jesus. All that's left for us to do is humbly, graciously and thankfully accept what Jesus has done on our behalf and put our faith in His finished work to save us.

That's what Jesus did by His life, death and resurrection. God set an impossible task that no man could fulfil when He gave the Law of Moses. But though we could never meet its demands and therefore never hope to earn eternal life by our own efforts, Jesus could. He came down beside us, lived a perfect life, fulfilled the requirements of the law and then died on our behalf shouting, "it is finished!" He fulfilled all the 613 requirements of the Law of Moses. He completed it on our behalf. And by completing it, that means there is nothing else for us to add. There's no credit we can claim. All we can do now is humbly, graciously and thankfully accept what Jesus has already done for us and put our faith in His finished work. And that's what makes the old Law of Moses obsolete.

Hebrews 8 says:

If the first covenant had been faultless, there would have been no need for a second covenant to replace it. But when God found fault with the people, he said:

> *"The day is coming, says the LORD,*
> *when I will make a new covenant*
> *with the people of Israel and Judah.*
> *This covenant will not be like the one*
> *I made with their ancestors*
> *when I took them by the hand*
> *and led them out of the land of Egypt.*
> *They did not remain faithful to my covenant,*
> *so I turned my back on them, says the LORD.*
> *But this is the new covenant I will make*
> *with the people of Israel on that day, says the LORD:*
> *I will put my laws in their minds,*
> *and I will write them on their hearts.*
> *I will be their God,*
> *and they will be my people.*
> *And they will not need to teach their neighbours,*
> *nor will they need to teach their relatives,*
> *saying, 'You should know the LORD.'*

For everyone, from the least to the greatest,
will know me already.
And I will forgive their wickedness,
and I will never again remember their sins."

When God speaks of a "new" covenant, it means he has made the first one obsolete. It is now out of date and will soon disappear." – Hebrews 8

Here the Hebrews writer is saying, *"you know that prophecy God made through Jeremiah all those centuries ago about a new covenant? A new covenant that would replace the Law of Moses? Well, Jesus is it. And the old covenant that was made when they came out of Egypt is now out of date and obsolete."* God had always planned to make the Law of Moses obsolete and to bring in a new dispensation of time. Paul writes, *"The law was our guardian until Christ came; it protected us until we could be made right with God through faith."* (Gal 3:24) The Law of Moses was a temporary measure until we could be made right through simple faith in Christ.

I've heard people argue that because Jesus kept to the Law of Moses, so should Christians. Listen to Paul when he writes, *"when the right time came, God sent his son, born of a woman, subject to the law. God sent him to buy freedom for us who were slaves to the law, so that he could adopt us as his very own children."* (Gal 4:4-5) Jesus had to live subject to the Law of Moses so that He could fulfil it and thereby set us free from it. That's the very reason he came! He lived under it to fulfil it so that we don't have to!

Later on the Hebrews writer says, *"He cancels the first covenant in order to establish the second…Under the old covenant the priest stands before the altar day by day, offering sacrifices that can never take away sins. But our High Priest [Jesus] offered himself to God as one sacrifice for sins, good for all time."*(Heb 10:9, 11)

Paul writes, *"By his death [Jesus] ended the whole system of Jewish law with its commandments and regulations..."* (Eph 2:15)

So we're reading over and over again that the entire Law of Moses has been cancelled or ended by its fulfilment in Jesus. That means that all 613 rules, the ten commandments included, are obsolete. This is a shock to many Christians who believe that the ten commandments should still play a central role. This is particularly a shock to the many legalists who still insist on living by the Law of Moses. And I imagine those people will be making some objections right about now. So I will attempt to anticipate those objections and to answer them.

IS THE LAW OF MOSES REALLY GONE?

The main argument against the idea of the Law of Moses being laid aside comes from Jesus' sermon on the mount when He said, *"Don't misunderstand why I have come. I did not come to abolish the law of Moses or the writings of the prophets. No, I have come to accomplish their purpose."* (Matt 5:17) The word 'abolish' here is the Greek work *kataluo* and it means "to disintegrate, demolish, overthrow or destroy". The word for 'accomplish' here is the Greek word *pleroo* which means "fill, make full, supply fully, complete." The difference between destroying (*kataluo*) and fulfilling (*pleroo*) is the difference between tearing up a mortgage contract and throwing it in the fire and paying the mortgage off in full. Both bring the mortgage to an end, but in vastly different ways. Jesus brought the law to a full conclusion by *pleroo*. He ended it by its completion. Which is the lawful way. And because He accomplished the law's purpose, He made it obsolete. After all, you don't keep paying into a mortgage that has already been paid off, right? Jesus paid our debt in full.

OK, but what about when Jesus said, *"I tell you the truth, until heaven and earth disappear, not even the smallest detail of God's law will disappear until its purpose is achieved."*? (Matt 5:18) Well, if the law will disappear when it's purpose is achieved then the question we have to ask ourselves is, "was its purpose achieved?" Romans 10:4 tells us, *"Christ has already accomplished the purpose for which the law was given."* So yes, the Law of Moses has disappeared!

Jesus was saying that the law's permanence was conditional and it could be brought to an end in one of two ways - either when heaven and earth ended or when its purpose had been achieved. It's like when a parent tells their child, *"you'll sit here all night unless you eat your peas."* The implication is that the child won't be there all night because they'll have eaten their peas by then. In the same way, Jesus would fulfil it before earth and heaven passed away. People focus so hard on the first condition that they miss the second. Jesus uses the same kind of phrasing in Matthew 24:34 and Luke 21:31-33.

OK, but what about when Jesus said, *"unless your righteousness exceeds that of the scribes and Pharisees, you will never enter the kingdom of heaven"?* (Matt 5:20) Doesn't that mean we have to try harder to keep the Law of Moses even better than they did? No. We just can't do it. *"No one is righteous - not even one."* (Rom 3:10) And it leads to cold, hard-hearted, hypocritical legalism when we try. We must learn this lesson so we don't repeat the Pharisee's mistakes. Remember the key phrase, *'the LORD is our righteousness'*. It is only through faith in Christ and His finished work that we can be considered righteous in God's sight. Not through anything we can do. God the Just is satisfied to look on *Him* and pardon me. We are wasting our time to try to make ourselves right with God through our own good works.

Some legalists will still argue that Jesus only made the Oral Law of the Pharisees obsolete but the written Law of Moses still stands. The main problem with this argument is that God never instituted the man-made Oral Law in the first place, so it could never be made obsolete. It was in sense, always obsolete. It was never useful. It was never God-ordained. You can't end something that was never in play in the first place, in the same way you can't pay off a mortgage that doesn't exist.

But what about when the Bible says that *"All Scripture is inspired by God and is useful to teach us what is true..."* (2 Tim 3:16) If *all* scripture is still useful that includes the Law of Moses, right? The Law of Moses is part of scripture. It must still have a purpose. Now *that's* correct. Now we're getting somewhere. It does have a use, and Paul defines its use when he says, *"We know that the law is good when used correctly. For the law was not intended for the righteous."* Who are the righteous again? The only people who can claim righteousness before God are Christians through faith in Jesus. *"The LORD is our righteousness"*. So the LAW OF MOSES is *not* intended for Christians.

Well what's its present day use then? Who is it for? Paul goes on, *"[The Law] is for people who are lawless and rebellious, who are ungodly and sinful, who consider nothing sacred and defile what is holy, who kill their father or mother or commit other murders. The law is for people who are sexually immoral, or who practice homosexuality, or are slave traders, liars, promise breakers, or who do anything else that contradicts the wholesome teaching that comes from the glorious Good News entrusted to me by our blessed God."* (1 Tim 1:8-11)

In other words the law is for unrepentant sinners. Remember, the one thing that law *can* do well is show people the difference between right and wrong. It can show people what Absolute Good looks like, thereby revealing their sin. It can show them what Absolute Light looks like, thereby revealing their darkness. It can show them what a Good Apple looks like, thereby reveal their rotten core. It can show them what a straight line looks like, thereby revealing their crookedness. As Paul puts it so simply, *"the law showed me my sin."* (Rom 7:7)

The law can't make people hate their sin or have any desire for God but it can at least bring them out of ignorance as to what sin is. The Law of Moses can still be used in a very basic way to show people that they fall short of God's perfect moral standard. But as soon as that sinner sees their sin, repents, and puts their faith in Jesus Christ as their Lord and Saviour, they have become righteous in God's sight and the law's usefulness for that person is finished. Their sin no longer condemns them because Jesus has already paid their debt in full and their hope of righteousness is in him alone. (Rom 8:1)

I have to labour this point because I know how many objections there are going to be. So many Christians have been brought up to believe that the Law of Moses still binds them and consequently they have mixed legalism with the faith. In the most extreme cases they have reduced Christianity to a list of legalistic thou shalts and shalt nots. But let me say this as clearly as I can now. The Law of Moses is obsolete. It has been cancelled. It has ended. It was fulfilled on our behalf by Jesus. That means even the ten commandments have gone. The ten commandments were just part of a single indivisible law that has been ended by its fulfilment in Jesus.

David Pawson writes about Christian ignorance in this area saying, *"I am amazed at how often I go into churches in this country and see the Ten Commandments displayed on the wall. The first church in England that I became pastor of in 1954 had the commandments up on the wall behind my head in chocolate-brown Gothic lettering! I decided that the first thing I was going to do was to paint it out, and so I got a pot of paint and painted all over it. There was a great outcry. Somebody complained that there was nothing to read during the sermon! They said they had to have something there, so I put up a cross on the wall instead"* (Unlocking the Bible p983)

Painting over the Law of Moses with the cross is actually a great picture of what happened. Our hope isn't in our ability to obey commands but in what Jesus did at Calvary. And when we understand that the whole Law of Moses has become obsolete, it instantly clears up so much confusion.

COMMON CONFUSION

For example, the group called the Seventh Day Adventists have made a whole faith system *centred* around the keeping of just one commandment - the 4th one. This is the one that says to keep the Saturday Sabbath. Their false prophetess, Ellen G White believed that keeping the Sabbath was so important that it was necessary for salvation. She said, *"I saw that the Holy Sabbath is, and will be, a separating wall between the true Israel of God and unbelievers."* (Early Writings p.33) So what she was saying is that if you're not going to keep the Saturday Sabbath, you can forget about eternal life. This is the kind of legalistic striving that Jesus came to set us free from! Yet even those outside of the SDAs can surprisingly make a big deal out of keeping the Sabbath.

But if you are relying on the day you worship to make yourself right with God then you better make sure you are keeping the other 612 laws perfectly too. Otherwise you're no better off than someone who keeps none of the laws. You are in fact putting yourself under the old Law of Moses with its curse of death and treating Jesus' cross as meaningless. Jesus can't help you if you're still relying on your own effort.

The abolition of the Law of Moses also answers the mockers who like to quote verses from the Old Testament in an attempt to discredit Christianity. They quote Leviticus 11:10 and say Christians should be banned from eating shellfish and that we're hypocritical for speaking against any sin as long as we continue to eat clams or lobster. Or they quote Deuteronomy 22:11 and say that before we speak up against homosexuality we should make sure we aren't wearing clothes woven from two types of material. In other words, they claim Christians are hypocrites for not following the strict dietary and clothing rules of the Law of Moses and claim we quote selectively from the Bible.

Of course, if they took the time to understand that the Law of Moses was made obsolete by Christ, they would understand that there is no hypocrisy whatsoever. Christians are not bound by the old law. We are completely free from those old rules that governed Israel.

That's not to say the Old Testament laws don't still contain some good principles - you still might want to think about cutting pork and shellfish out of your diet - but there is no law against it.

I heard Stephen Fry say on an episode of QI that the Bible was confused because it told people to turn the other cheek and forgive enemies but also told them to take an eye for an eye. Of course the 'eye for an eye' instruction belonged to the old Law of Moses which governed Israel in Old Testament times and has been made obsolete. There is no conflict.

So what am I saying then? That there's no such thing as morality for Christians now? That we can do whatever we want? That we live under lawlessness?   No. Remember what we learned before. If you take a civil law away...

The eternal, unchanging, moral law that underpins it remains:

The MORAL LAW *never* changes. Civil laws are variable but the MORAL LAW is eternal. So even though the Law of Moses...

is taken away...

the MORAL LAW that underpins it remains. The Law of Moses was a temporary expression of something much deeper and long-lasting.

So you see, it was wrong to murder *before* we had the Law of Moses, it was wrong to murder *during* the Law of Moses and it's wrong to murder *after* the Law of Moses has ended. The rightness and wrongness of things don't depend on the existence of the Law of Moses.

Similarly, it was wrong to steal *before* the Law of Moses, *during* the Law of Moses, and *after* the Law of Moses.

To prove this point, think of Cain and Abel. Cain murdered Abel at the beginning of Genesis, well *before* the Law of Moses had been given, but God still punished Cain because the eternal MORAL LAW was always in effect. Paul writes, *"Yes, people sinned even before the law [of Moses] was given. And though there was no law to break, since it had not yet been given, they all died anyway."* (Rom 5:13-14) God's MORAL LAW never changes and is completely unaffected by the ending of the Law of Moses. If something *was* immoral, it always *will be* immoral.

Furthermore, remember what Hebrews said: *"He cancels the first covenant in order to establish the second ..."* The end of the old covenant doesn't mean that there's no covenant at all. It just means it has been replaced with a better one. We live in a new way under a new dispensation of time and a new law. This law is called The Law of Christ, The Royal Law or The Spirit Life.

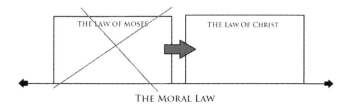

THE LAW OF MOSES   THE LAW OF CHRIST

THE MORAL LAW

We'll explore what the new era looks like next.

CHAPTER 11
THE NEW WAY

Paul wrote to the Corinthians saying, *"The old way, with its laws etched in stone, led to death, though it began with such glory that people could not bear to look at Moses' face. For his face shone with the glory of God, even though the brightness was already fading away. Shouldn't we expect far greater glory under the new way, now that the Holy Spirit is giving life? If the old way, which brings condemnation, was glorious, how much more glorious is the new way, which makes us right with God! In fact, that first glory was not glorious at all compared with the overwhelming glory of the new way. So if the old way, which has been replaced, was glorious, how much more glorious is the new, which remains forever!" (2 Corinthians 3:7-11)*

Paul confirms here that the Law of Moses was an old way that has faded, was set aside and was replaced with a new way that will remain forever.

What is this new way?

It's the spirit life of Christ that began when the Law of Moses ended. And it's centred around a single law.

THE SERMON ON THE MOUNT

Jesus introduced His law in the sermon on the mount - the sermon which is universally recognised as the most sublime piece of moral teaching ever given. And when we examine this sermon we find Jesus strongly emphasising that He's not looking for a change in outward behaviour or adherence to laws as much as He's looking for a change of heart. For example, He tells the people, *"You have heard that our ancestors were told, "You must not murder. If you commit murder you are subject to judgement. But I say, if you are even angry with someone you are subject to judgement!"* (Matt 5:21-22) Likewise He goes on to say, *"You have heard the commandment that says, "You must not commit adultery. But I say, anyone who even looks at a woman with lust has already committed adultery with her in his heart."* (Matt 5:27-28)

What Jesus is saying here is, *"I'm not so interested in your external actions; I'm interested in the corruption of your heart. Even though you don't go ahead and commit the adultery, just the fact you have those lustful desires in your heart speaks of its corruption. Even though you don't go ahead and murder, just the fact you have that anger in your heart speaks of its corruption."* Jesus is looking deeper than what people do. He's looking at what they think and feel and desire. He's judging motives. He's looking at hearts. Remember, he came to heal the inherent heart sickness.

Jesus contrasts his teaching with the old law *("You have heard it said...but I say...")*, and by doing so, He was actually highlighting that the old law was morally inferior. He was saying that the end of the ten commandments didn't mean lawlessness...it meant that we were now going to be held to an even *higher* standard.

For example, under the Ten Commandments someone could foster a deep hatred for a foreigner and fantasise about killing him, but as long as he didn't act on the thought and commit the murder, he technically wasn't breaking the law. The sixth commandment only judged the action, not the thought. This allowed for duplicitousness of heart and inner moral decay to set in. It allowed for people to become unwashed cups and whitewashed tombs - seemingly good on the outside but full of hate and anger inside. But here, under the new way being announced by Jesus, that possibility was gone. Jesus was saying, *"you could do that under the old way, but I don't just want new actions...I want new hearts."*

Jesus said this knowing that new hearts would automatically lead to the required good actions.

So apart from anything else, anyone who insists on clinging onto the ten commandments or the Law of Moses, is actually holding to an inferior moral code than those who have gone on to accept and live under the new covenant.

We can go on with similar examples of how the Ten Commandments is morally inferior:

The Law of Moses had said to love just your neighbour; the Law of Christ goes further and says to love enemies too.

The Law of Moses had said you can divorce one another with just a written note; the Law of Christ goes further and says there are only a very small number of specific circumstances when divorce is allowed at all.

Jesus wasn't lowering the bar in any way; he was raising it.

THE LAW OF CHRIST

At the end of His sermon on the mount Jesus then gives the simple command that sums up everything He wants to say (key verses in bold):

*"**Do to others whatever you would like them to do to you.** This is the essence of all that is taught in the law and the prophets"* (Matt 7:12)

Later in His ministry He repeats, *"**'You must love the LORD your God with all your heart, all your soul, and all your mind.' This is the first and greatest commandment. A second is equally important: 'Love your neighbour as yourself.'** The entire law and all the demands of the prophets are based on these two commandments."* (Matt 22:36-40)

He says it again, *"I have loved you even as the Father has loved me. Remain in my love. When you obey my commandments, you remain in my love, just as I obey my Father's commandments and remain in his love. I have told you these things so that you will be filled with my joy. Yes, your joy will overflow!* **This is my commandment: Love each other in the same way I have loved you."** *(John 15:9-12)*

And again: **"So now I am giving you a new commandment: Love each other. Just as I have loved you, you should love each other.** *Your love for one another will prove to the world that you are my disciples."* (John 13:34-35)

Later on John would write, **"And this is his commandment: We must believe in the name of his Son, Jesus Christ, and love one another, just as he commanded us.** *Those who obey God's commandments remain in fellowship with him, and he with them."* (1 John 3:23-24)

So here is the new commandment or the Law of Christ:

1. Put your faith in Christ, love God with all your heart, soul and mind and love others as yourself.

And that's it! Faith and selfless love. It really can't get much simpler!

Think about it and you'll see the genius of this. If you love God with all your heart, soul and mind you won't worship other gods or turn away from him or blaspheme His name and you'll be careful to serve Him and follow His decrees. And if you love others as yourself you won't murder them, steal from them, lie to them, injure them, be jealous of them or commit adultery...in fact you won't even foster those thoughts in your hearts. So by following the Law of Christ you will automatically fulfil the MORAL LAW. Love therefore, is the key.

The apostle Paul writes, *"Owe nothing to anyone—except for your obligation to love one another. If you love your neighbour, you will fulfill the requirements of God's law. For the commandments say, "You must not commit adultery. You must not murder. You must not steal. You must not covet." These— and other such commandments—are summed up in this one commandment: "Love your neighbour as yourself." Love does no wrong to others, so love fulfills the requirements of God's law."* (Rom 13:8-10)

In his letter to the Galatians he also writes, *"...the whole law can be summed up by this one command: "Love your neighbour as yourself."* (Gal 5:14)

James refers to this new law as the ROYAL LAW saying, *"Yes indeed, it is good when you obey the royal law as found in the Scriptures: "Love your neighbour as yourself."* (Jam 2:8)

Jesus didn't leave us with no law at all. He simply gave us a better one - put your faith in Christ for salvation and love God and love one another. And that's it. There are no more rules beyond that. None.

THE LAW OF CHRIST IN ACTION

What might people who love God and others before themselves look like? The New Testament is full of examples.

Loving God

If we love God it means we trust Him with our lives; it means we try to get to know him better; it means we show our gratitude towards him and never forget Him as the source of our blessing; we worship him and praise him; it means we joyfully serve him; pray to him; live in accordance with His will; walk by His leading; hold fast to the truth about him and defend it in public; tell others about what Jesus has done; do everything in life for His glory and be diligent in our devotion and study of His word. It means we don't entertain idols, we don't let anything replace him in our affections, we don't give position to false teachers who skew the word of God and we don't mock, blaspheme or speak against him.

Love Others

If we love others that means we love not just those who love us, but our enemies too; it means showing compassion and sympathy and even sharing in the suffering of others; it means being forgiving and forbearing; it means dealing honestly and fairly with everyone and never cheating anyone; it means doing good to all and helping everyone where we can; it means telling the truth; it means being courteous and trying to live at peace with everyone; it means treating others like we would want them to treat us; it means providing a good example and it means urging one another to do good deeds and to help those who are falling away from the faith. It also means never lying, never stealing, committing murder, committing adultery or fornication, speaking evil of others or being what the Bible calls 'unequally yoked' in marriage. It means working out disputes with each other in private and staying debt free. You know what? It looks like even smaller things than these. It looks like holding doors open for one another, saying please and thank you, sending flowers, it looks like simple good manners.

The beauty of this new law is that you are not restricted by a specific set of rules on how you love God and others. Instead, you are free to express your love spontaneously, authentically and extravagantly in any way you can imagine. Hebrews 10:24 says, *"Let us think of ways to motivate one another to acts of love and good works."* In other words, *"let's see how inventive and imaginative we can be in loving one another."* Some translations use the phrase *"outbursts of love and good works"*. Love should bursting out of us so that we're unrestrictedly lavish with it. We can never go too far in loving God or others.

Mutual Submission

The Bible takes time to describe what our personal relationships should look like when all parties are intent on selflessly loving one another like this.

It says that when you love others you naturally put their needs ahead of your own. Therefore it calls us to submit to one another.

It tells us wives should lovingly submit to their husbands and that husbands should lovingly put his wife's needs ahead of his own to the extent that he would give up his own life for her

(Eph 5:21-33). A lot is made of wives being taught to submit to their husbands in Christian teaching but the second part is equally important - husbands are to be 'servant leaders' by putting her needs first.

In the same way, the Bible tells children to be obedient to parents and parents not to be harsh with their children but to do what's best for them. (Eph 6:1-4). Again, put each other first out of love.

This also means that employees serve their bosses sincerely with their hardest and most honest work and it means that the employer treats the employee well, with dignity and respect, looking after their needs. (Eph 6:5-9)

Servant Leadership

In other words, love for one another introduces us to the principle of mutual submission which means those under authority submit to that authority willingly and those in authority use it to serve rather than rule.

Jesus was the first example of *servant leadership* - it was a revolutionary concept. Remember when Jesus knelt down to wash His disciples feet? The Bible says, *"After washing their feet, he put on his robe and sat down and asked, 'Do you understand what I was doing? You call me 'Teacher' and 'Lord' and you are right, because that's what I am. And since I, your Lord and Teacher, have washed your feet, you ought to wash each other's feet. I have given you an example to follow. Do as I have done to you...God will bless you for [it]."* (John 13:12-17)

So even though Jesus was their Lord and had authority over them, He used His position to serve them. Likewise husbands, though they have authority over wives, serve their wives. Parents, though they have authority over children, serve them. Bosses, though they have authority over employees, serve them. In exchange the wives, children and employees submit willingly and lovingly to Godly leadership. This is how we create harmonious homes, workplaces and societies.

This servant leadership concept is the origin of the idea that our politicians and public officials are elected to serve us rather than to rule over us too. In fact, we call our elected officials, *public servants* and this idea finds its origin in Jesus' revolutionary teaching. The concept is that we elect them so that they can serve us and in return, we willingly submit to their leadership.

Of course, as Jesus is marginalised from society, we're seeing this concept being eroded too. Government leaders are increasingly power grabbing, dictatorial and acting out of self-interest. This is evidenced almost daily by corruption scandals.

But when we put this concept of Christ-like mutual submission into practice, out of love for one another, it is the most beautiful thing imaginable. It causes peace and harmony and the more good you do for others the more good they will do for you. In this way, love multiplies.

THE HOLY SPIRIT IS KEY

Now wait a minute. This all sounds amazing but...what about our heart sickness?

I mean, it's all very well Jesus giving us a command to love God and each other and then giving us a sublime expression of the MORAL LAW to follow... but what chance of following it do we have with these old sinful natures? What about the age-old problem of moral entropy?

If we couldn't keep the Law of Moses because of an inherent tendency to lean towards sin, why would we be any better at keeping the Law of Christ? And if we naturally veer towards selfishness, how on earth are we going to have any chance of living a life where we put God and others first? There's no point giving us a law which is a fuller and higher expression of God's character if we couldn't keep the old inferior law. That's just giving these unregenerate hearts a new law to break, right? We need the internal healing.

And didn't God promise that He would deal with our heart sickness through Jesus? Didn't He say through the prophets, *"And I will give you a new heart, and I will put a new spirit in you. I will take out your stony, stubborn heart and give you a tender, responsive heart. And I will put my Spirit in you so that you will follow my decrees and be careful to obey my regulations."? (Ezekiel 36:26-27)*

He did.

So before Jesus left the earth, He gave this command to His disciples: *"Do not leave Jerusalem until the Father sends you the gift he has promised, as I told you before. John baptised with water, but in just a few days, you will be baptised with the Holy Spirit...you will receive power when the Holy Spirit comes upon you. And you will be my witnesses, telling people about me everywhere - in Jerusalem, through Judea, in Samaria, and to the ends of the earth."* (Acts 1:4,5,8)

Jesus was going to send His followers the long promised Holy Spirit which would come and indwell them. This was the Spirit that God promised through Ezekiel when He said, *"And I will put my Spirit in you...."* It would be this Spirit that would empower them, regenerate their hearts, give them new desires, new convictions. It would be the Spirit of Christ within them. And it would cure the heart sickness. It would cause them to love good.

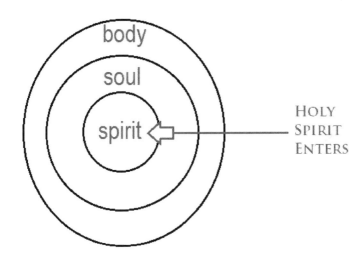

With the Holy Spirit within our hearts we would no longer be subject to the moral entropy of sin. Instead, we would undergo a reversal of that process called *sanctification*. Paul writes that, *"Even though our outward man is perishing, yet the inward man is being renewed day by day."* (2 Cor 4:16) This just means although our external bodies are still dying - even though our flesh is still subject to entropy - our hearts are actually being regenerated through the power of the Spirit. Our hearts are no longer degrading and moving towards chaos and death; the power of Christ within us is moving them towards renewal and life. The arrival of the Holy Spirit in our hearts means we would constantly improve and grow and mature and become more righteous with each passing day. We would start to conform to the image of Jesus himself. His life within us would start to make us like him. With the Holy Spirit now controlling our hearts, at the core of our being, we would now be empowered to go after the MORAL LAW. To choose good. To crave good. To love good. We would no longer be slaves to sin. It would no longer control us. We would have a brand new nature.

The Holy Spirit would change everything.

The Holy Spirit *did* change everything.

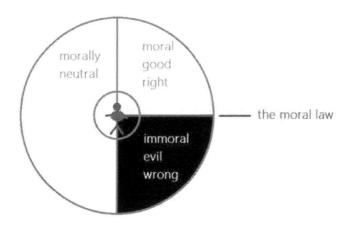

It's got to be noted that the process of sanctification is a very gradual thing that will continue for the rest of our lives. Sometimes we *do* find that our old desires for sin are instantly gone - that can happen. I have experienced it myself and I know others who can give similar accounts. Sometimes you *do* wake up one day and suddenly discover that something you once craved actually disgusts you. But more often than not, the process of sanctification is a very slow one.

You'll still experience temptations and you'll still have struggles. But the main difference is this...you'll now be empowered to say 'no'. Sin won't be able to overwhelm you in the way that it once did. You'll no longer be a slave to the sinful nature. Romans 8:26 says that the *"Holy Spirit helps us in our weakness."* 2 Corinthians 3:18 says, *"the spirit of the LORD makes us more and more like him as we are changed into his glorious image."* 2 Corinthians 5:14 says, *"Whatever we do, it is because Christ's love controls us."*

As Christ's love controls us through the Spirit, we increasingly find that our inner desires are changing. It's not just that we know what good and evil is better, but we begin to love good and hate evil. Jacquelyn Heasley said, *"it's one thing not to sin - it's another not to want to!"* Christians increasingly find themselves in the latter camp - they don't just force themselves to stop sinning, although an act of the will is involved - they begin not to *want* to. Things they used to love they begin to hate and things they used to hate they now love. Christians, in a sense, turn into brand new men and women. That's why we often use the term, 'born again'. We become new creations.

WHAT SANCTIFICATION LOOKS LIKE

What are some of the specifics that you might experience through sanctification?

Well, you'll develop an appetite for God's word and as you read the Bible, the Holy Spirit within you will illuminate your mind, giving you insight into truths that previously made no sense. In this way you'll grow in knowledge and wisdom. Your thoughts will come out of the gutter and your speech will clear up too. Swearing and cursing will no longer trip off your tongue. You'll develop humility. Your ambitions will change and you'll no longer be so focused on worldly wealth, fame, pleasures or esteem. You'll become more content with what you have. You'll find a deeper sense of joy and peace. Your conscience will become sharper so things you once thought were ok will now bother you. Your improved knowledge of good will give you an acute perception of evil. You'll use your time more wisely. You'll be entertained by different things. You'll find yourself becoming different from many of the people around you. You'll stop conforming to the pattern of the world. You'll want to do useful work and to help people more. You'll quite possibly want to look after your body more. You'll let go of anger, resentment and unforgiveness. You'll worry less. You'll make better choices. You'll stop being lazy. Death will no longer scare you.

The Bible has the best list of the benefits that you should see from having the Spirit living inside you. They're called the *Fruits of the Spirit*. Paul wrote, *"But the Holy Spirit produces this kind of fruit in our lives: love, joy, peace, patience, kindness, goodness, faithfulness, gentleness, and self-control. There is no law against these things!" (Galatians 5:22-23)*

That's the kind of person you will become. And that's all from the power of the Holy Spirit inside. A heart that was once calloused, stony and unresponsive to God will start to come to life again. Paul wrote, *"The Spirit of God, who raised Jesus from the dead, lives in you. And just as God raised Christ Jesus from the dead, he will give life to your mortal bodies by this same Spirit living within you." (Rom 8:11)*

It'll become tender and responsive again. It'll come to life. Bit by bit.

Of course, you will retain your free-will so you will still need to follow the Spirit's leading. And in my experience that process works like this:

God will show you something that needs to change through your conscience/spirit. If you are obedient and act upon that leading and make the change, God will then show you something else. If you act upon that too, God will show you something more. Oswald Chambers wrote, *"Obey God in the thing he shows you, and instantly the next thing is opened up. God will never reveal more truth about himself until you have obeyed what you know already."* When you take these little steps of obedience, before long you will find yourself looking back and being shocked at how much you have changed. How much you now abhor things that used to be attractive. Your increasing understanding of light helps you understand how dark you used to be. Follow the leading of the Holy Spirit and he will gradually transform you inwardly into a new person. I wish I could describe it better for you but you really have to experience it for yourself. The key is just to be obedient to the thing He shows you, no matter how big or small, how confusing or how clear cut the direction seems to be. Just act in faith by following the voice of the Spirit. The fruit of the spirit will soon follow.

FOLLOWING THE SPIRIT

Every time you respond with obedience to the Holy Spirit, you are following the Law of Christ because you're telling God that His will comes first.

Remember the Law of Christ is simply, have faith in Christ then love God and others before yourself. Think of yourself last. When you follow the leading of the Spirit you are putting God first.

When you ignore the voice of the Spirit however and put yourself first, you're telling God that He comes second to your own selfish desires. And as we know, 'do what *you* want' is the Law of Satan. The Law of Satan is an inversion of the Law of Christ.

Simply, the Law of Satan is **selfish** (yourself first); the Law of Christ is **selfless** (God and others first).

Every moral choice you make is a straight one between Jesus' path and Satan's path. Every time you put God or others ahead of yourself out of love, you're following the lead of the Holy Spirit, fulfilling the Law of Christ, and killing the sinful nature. Every time you put yourself first, you are hardening yourself to the voice of God and giving more strength to the sin within you.

So at this very moment in your life there is something you know you should change. Do it. Make the change. Be ruthless with your sinful nature. Let Christ's influence and power grow inside you. Let him guide your decisions and let him transform you inwardly into the likeness of Jesus himself.

THE LAW OF CHRIST IS BETTER THAN THE LAW OF MOSES

Hopefully we're starting to get a glimpse of how much better life is under the Law of Christ compared to life under the Law of Moses. Instead of hundreds of oppressive rules that we can never keep, we have just one. Love! Jesus has taken the heavy burden of the Law of Moses off our shoulders and given us a very easy and simple way of living. That's why He says, *"Come to me, all of you who are weary and carry heavy burdens, and I will give you rest. Take my yoke upon you. Let me teach you, because I am humble and gentle at heart, and you will find rest for your souls. For my yoke is easy to bear, and the burden I give you is light."*(Matt 11:28-30) His yoke is easy and His burden is light because He asks just one thing. Have faith in Him then love God and one other. No burdensome mountains of rules. No lists of thou shalts and shalt nots.

They're not required because the Holy Spirit now empowers us to *choose* the MORAL LAW. To crave goodness. To do the right thing when no one is looking. We're regulated by the Spirit's power within so we don't need mountains of laws trying to coerce us from without. We use our freedom to do good.

Still not keen to leave behind the Law Of Moses? Still keen to burden people with legalism? Paul has a word of warning for you: *"This is a covenant, not of written laws, but of the Spirit. The old written covenant ends in death; but under the new covenant, the Spirit gives life."* (2 Cor 3:6) Paul is saying that if we insist on holding to the old way it will not end well for us...it ends in death...and we'll become Pharisaic in the process. If you want to live by the Spirit you must let go of the old written law.

Paul goes on to talk about those who refuse to give up the old covenant saying that their minds have been covered with a veil. He says, *"But the people's minds were hardened, and to this day whenever the old covenant is being read, the same veil covers their minds so they cannot understand the truth. And this veil can be removed only by believing in Christ. Yes, even today when they read Moses' writings, their hearts are covered with that veil, and they do not understand.*

But whenever someone turns to the Lord, the veil is taken away. For the Lord is the Spirit, and wherever the Spirit of the Lord is, there is freedom. So all of us who have had that veil removed can see and reflect the glory of the Lord. And the

Lord—who is the Spirit—makes us more and more like him as we are changed into his glorious image." (2 Cor 3:14-18)

If you are chained to the Law of Moses in your mind then ask for Jesus to give you His Spirit and to remove the veil. Instead, let life in the Spirit and love for one another under the Law of Christ be our hallmark as Christians.

CHAPTER 12
CHRIST BRINGS FREEDOM

I want to really press home just how much freedom we have in Christ now. Because up until now our focus has been on how the Spirit helps us choose between good and evil. In other words, our focus has been on the right hand side of the diagram.

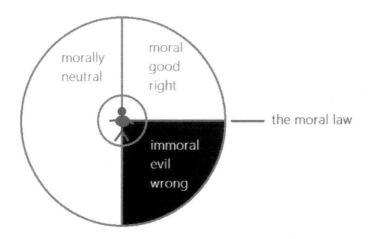

But we haven't said much about how the Law of Christ affects our relationship with morally *neutral* things - we haven't looked much at the left side of the diagram. And that's very important too.

You see, under the Law of Moses there were all these strict rules about morally neutral things: what people could eat, drink, what they could wear, what day they had to worship etc.

But Jesus took all those rules away. This happened:

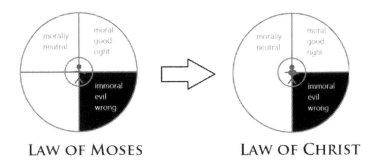

LAW OF MOSES   LAW OF CHRIST

That bar across the morally neutral issues on the left - that bar that created rights and wrongs on what people could eat, drink and wear was taken away.

"Have faith in Jesus then love God and others before yourself" says nothing about whether you're ok to eat lobster or mushrooms. In fact, the Law of Christ says nothing specific about neutral things at all. All those rules are taken away.

What it *does* give us, however, is a new *mindset* to work with.

How do we fulfil the Law of Christ with morally neutral things? How do we show faith in Christ while loving God and others with neutral things? With food, drink and clothing? How do we love God and others with all the things we listed at the start of this book? With wood, grass, cotton, metal, stone, vegetables, plants, earth, trains, musical instruments, shoes, hats, dinners, computers, footballs, plastic chairs, wooden chairs, barbecues, television sets, windows, airplanes, money, stuffed animals, toothpaste and light bulbs?

Well...that's now up to you. You're free.

You are now free to offer love authentically, spontaneously and extravagantly.

What I mean is, God doesn't so much care *how* you love people with those things - he doesn't care so much about what the external actions look like - as much as he cares about the fact that every action you take is rooted in a heartfelt desire to love Him and love other people ahead of yourself, and in doing so, fulfil the Law of Christ.

As Paul puts it, *"whether you eat or drink, or whatever you do, do it all for the glory of God."*(1 Cor 10:31) Just do what you do for the right reasons. The internal is more important than the external. Follow the voice of the Spirit. Listen to your conscience. Act on His prompts. Be selfless.

Let's take money as an example. Money is a neutral thing. It's not inherently good or evil. It's just metal and paper and plastic. So it belongs firmly in the left hand side of our diagram. Now under the old Law of Moses, there were specific rules on such things. People were required to give 10% of their income to the temple.

Now, however, that law is taken away and we're simply told to love God and others with what we have. So how we do that is up to us. We could donate the money to charity, we could buy a homeless person some clothes or food, we could buy flowers for our significant other, we could add it to an extra generous tip at lunch, we could sponsor someone, we could buy someone a Bible...in fact the ways in which we can use our money to express love are almost endless. We can be as inventive as we want. And God says that it doesn't matter which way you choose; what matters is that you're acting on His prompts via

His Spirit and doing it all for His glory. He's looking at your heart. That's the freedom we have. It frees us to be authentic, extravagant and spontaneous. It means we don't have to stick to 10% to meet a law either. We can give 15% or 20% or 100% because we can never be too loving.

With morally neutral things, all that matters is the motive. Are you putting God and others first? Then you're fulfilling the Law of Christ.

THE MOTIVE MATTERS MORE

Now this principle has surprising consequences, because it means it's possible for two people to perform *the exact same external action*, and for God to *love* one act and *hate* the other.

For example, two men may give money to charity - the external action is the same for both men - but while the first man is motivated by genuine love and he does it so discreetly that no one even notices the donation was made, the second man makes a show in public of his generosity and hopes to receive praise for it. In this case, the external action is the same, but their motivations are entirely different. The first man is donating out of genuine love for others while the second man is donating for his own selfish glory and pride. Therefore, God loves the first donation but he hates the second. Because only the first man was really following the Law of Christ. The second was doing it for selfish reasons. He was actually following the Law of Satan! So it's actually possible to give to charity sinfully! We must always be examining our own hearts.

We can see this in the gospel of Mark where Jesus is sitting near the collection box in the Temple watching as the rich people made a show of the large amounts they were donating (Mark

12:41-44). They dropped vast sums of money into the box and Jesus was completely unimpressed. Why? Because they were only doing it to glorify themselves. Their motivation was self-centred pride. However, when a poor widow came in and subtly dropped 2 measly small coins into the box and tried to sneak away unseen, Jesus' heart melted and was quick to honour her. "See her", He told His disciples. "She's just given more than anyone." Her donation was the least in a strictly monetary sense but her motivation was the best. The rich people were only concerned about glorifying themselves but the widow was genuinely glorifying God so that's the one Jesus got excited about. He saw her heart.

The Bible says *"People judge by outward appearances but the LORD looks at the heart."* (1 Sam 16:7). Most people would look at the external actions of anyone giving to charity and be impressed with any contribution. But God is looking deeper. Again, following the Law of Christ is primarily a heart issue. He's interested in what you do to an extent but only inasmuch as it shows what's happening in your heart. He's interested in your inner transformation more than anything. Are you becoming Christ like? Are you following the leading of the Holy Spirit? Are you putting him and others first? Or are you actually just trying to make a name for yourself? God doesn't primarily want new external actions; He wants new people with renovated hearts. He wants you to become more selfless and less selfish. Putting others first is Christ-like. Putting yourself first is Satan-like.

John the Baptist led by example on this saying, *"He [Jesus] must become greater and greater and I must become less and less."* (John 3:30). The life of Christ must grow within our hearts through his Spirit and as it must destroy our pride and egocentrism. We must become less and less. In all you do ask yourself, 'am I doing this to glorify myself or God?' Jesus says that on the day of judgement a lot of people are going to come to him saying, *'don't you remember the time I did this for you? Don't you remember the time I did that for you?'* And Jesus will say, *'You did those things for your own glory. I never knew you'. (Matt 7:23)*

This is very important for those involved in Christian ministry. Are you up on the stage because you genuinely want to serve God and others or are you up there because you love the limelight? There's a sense in which our ministries, our worship, our preaching and even our good acts can become sinful in the sight of God if we are motivated by selfish pride. You might think you've spent your whole life in His service but really, if you're to be honest, it's always been about you. Be careful with that. You must be willing to make yourself nothing in the world's eyes in order to be everything in God's.

Paul writes to the Corinthians on this subject saying, *"So be careful not to jump to conclusions before the Lord returns as to whether or not someone is faithful. When the Lord comes, he will bring our deepest secrets to light and will reveal our private motives. And then God will give everyone whatever praise is due."* (1 Cor 4:5)

God will judge based on what motivated us. In neutral matters what we do is not as important as *why* we're doing it. Having been given freedom from the written law by Christ, we can now use that freedom in one of two ways - to serve ourselves or to serve others. If we're truly living by the Spirit, we'll use our freedom for others.

Therefore motivation is more important than action.

SWEARING

The principle of motivation mattering more than external actions has even further reaching consequences. For example, it explains why swearing is wrong.

Letters and words are neutral and therefore they belong in the left side of our diagram. As moral agents, we can take those words and manipulate them for good or evil. We can use them to love God and others, following the Law of Christ, or we can use them to tear down others, blaspheme God, and be selfish, following the Law of Satan.

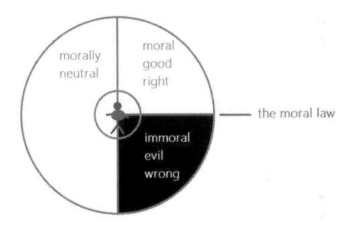

Let's take "the F word" as an example. It is four randomly arranged letters that make a certain sound. There is nothing moral about the letter "F" or any of the three letters that follow it. There's nothing inherently good about them and there's nothing inherently evil about them. There's nothing inherently good or evil about the arrangement of the letters either or the sound they make when spoken. It's completely neutral. Indeed, if the English language had developed differently those same four letters could easily have come to represent our word for something completely different. It could have been our word for "soup" or "tree" or "clouds". But as it is, what is the *motivation* behind our use of that word today?

When people use that word their *motivation* is to be abusive, crass, ugly, dirty, shocking and crude and thus, *that* is what makes it sinful for us to use. Because being abusive and crass is the complete antithesis of the Law of Christ. We are breaking Christ's law when we use such a word. The word itself is irrelevant really, it's what that word says about your heart.

Remember Jesus said that it's what comes out of you that makes you unclean (Matt 15:11)? He was teaching that what comes out of a person reveals inner motives and inner purity and that's what He's looking at. What's happening inside you? Is the Holy Spirit changing you? Sanctifying you? Or is there still enough selfish ugliness in there that it comes pouring out of your mouth like garbage when you talk? For the same reason, haughty boasting is just as bad as swearing. Our words when we are controlled by the Spirit should be humble, loving and designed to build others up.

BE AUTHENTIC, SPONTANEOUS & EXTRAVAGANT

So you see the freedom that Christ gave us. It wasn't just freedom to choose good over evil; it was freedom to use morally neutral things to be authentic, spontaneous and extravagant with our love.

He simply asks that we put faith in him, then love God and others...and leaves the rest up to us. How will we choose to express our faith in him? How will we choose to express our love for God and others? You decide.

Be authentic. If you like writing songs then write God a song. Or write someone you love a song. Be spontaneous. Give someone flowers. Give them your time. Give them a call. Give thanks to God before you eat your food. Be extravagant. Wash the neighbour's car. Go further than you need to. Babysit to let a couple have a night out. Dance for God. Drink that with thanksgiving, eat that with joy. It's up to you. Express your love freely, with thanksgiving and a clear conscience. Because you really are free now. Live by the Spirit and not the law. That is the liberty of the gospel.

A New Mindset

And this transition away from rule observance and ritual towards free, authentic, spontaneous and extravagant expressions of love should create a whole new mindset in Christians.

The question Christians often still ask is, *"what can I get away with? Can I get away with saying **** as a Christian? How much alcohol can I drink? How far can I push it with my girlfriend? What are the minimum requirements? Can I do that? What are the rules?"* If that's your attitude then you're only thinking of yourself and you're not living the Spirit life yet. You may as well still be under the old covenant.

Christians should be asking themselves a new set of questions. *"How can I excel in love? How can I go beyond the ordinary? How can I be extravagant in love? How can I encourage others to outbursts of love? What can I do that will be the best for others today? How can I be proactive? How can I authentically express my thankfulness to God in the best possible way?"*

In other words, no longer ask what you can get away with; ask how you can excel. Don't ask what minimum requirements the law asks of you; ask how you can be authentic, spontaneous and extravagant with your love. Let it come from the heart, let it be real and let it be liberal.

In fact, here's a little experiment that you can do today...

Rather than waiting for the next Valentine's Day, Christmas, a birthday or anniversary to come around to demand that you buy a gift for someone, just go out and do it now. Spontaneously. Don't wait for a social contract to demand you make an effort for others by 'law'. Go buy flowers or some other gift for your partner and make it a surprise. It doesn't have to be flowers and it doesn't have to be your husband or wife; just go do something spontaneously, extravagantly loving for another human being. Then watch what happens.

Watch how that generates joy and love in them. Watch how puzzled they become and the way they question your motives. If it's your husband or wife they might ask, *"What's the occasion? It's not our anniversary? It's not Valentine's Day? What have you done wrong?"* If they ask those questions it's a sad state of affairs because it means they're conditioned to only receiving gifts when you've been duty-bound to give them. And if that's the case you haven't really been showing Christ-like love for them.

Christians should never wait for 'law' to demand we give something of ourselves. It should be part of our every-day lifestyles. Giving freely should be the norm for us. And the truth is that love that isn't freely given isn't love at all; it's just duty. So we have to give freely if it's to be genuine.

It doesn't have to even be something that costs money either. Giving of your time is actually often worth far more. Just take time out with someone. Pray with someone. Ask them to share what's on their mind and take some of their load. Just take the principle of loving God and others authentically, spontaneously and extravagantly and let it soak into your heart so that every day you go to bed having done some good in the world. As you go through the day, if you feel a prompt by the Spirit to do some act of kindness, get into the habit of responding to those prompts immediately. Don't argue with God, just act. I will list some ideas for random acts of kindness in the Appendix to get you started but they should only be that - a starting point. The Bible exhorts us to think of new and imaginative ways to spur each other on to outbursts of love all the time.

And let me end this chapter by saying that if we behave in this way, I guarantee we will soon have the world's attention, because we will just be so refreshingly and shockingly different from the 99% of the world that people encounter every day.

"Few things are more infectious than a godly lifestyle. The people you rub shoulders with every day need that kind of challenge. Not prudish. Not preachy. Just crackerjack clean living. Just honest to goodness, bone-deep, non-hypocritical integrity." - Chuck Swindoll

The Law of Christ is simple, elegant, beautiful and life-changing.

"It is not what a man does that determines whether his work is sacred or secular, it is why he does it. The motive is everything." - A.W. Tozer

"Do all the good you can. By all the means you can. In all the ways you can. In all the places you can. At all the times you can.

To all the people you can. As long as ever you can." - John Wesley

CHAPTER 13
THE JUDAISERS

After Jesus had ascended to heaven and the Holy Spirit had been given, the apostles became empowered to spread the Gospel message far and wide. With the regenerating power of God within their hearts, they proclaimed the freedom from the law that was now possible through faith in Christ and many thousands of people accepted it.

Unfortunately, not everyone found it so easy to let go of the Law of Moses. The Jews had lived under the Law of Moses for so long that it had become a part of their whole cultural identity. Moses had always been their most revered prophet. Just letting all that go was more than some of them could accept.

What's more, whereas the Law of Moses had been just for the nation of Israel, the Law of Christ was opening up God's message to the entire world. There was a sudden influx of people into the faith from all over - people with no Jewish heritage or culture at all - from Asia, Africa and Europe. People that Israel has always considered to be pagan "Gentiles". As these Gentiles came into the faith, they had none of this Jewish heritage, absolutely no knowledge of the Law of Moses, and they were doing distinctly un-Jewish things. The Jews were a little put out by this. Many of them became jealous and angry.

It's a bit like when a new baby arrives in a household and the older siblings who have been around a while are put out because suddenly they aren't the sole focus of attention anymore. Basically, the Jews couldn't believe God wanted to accept these awful pagans from surrounding nations.

God made it clear to them that He was accepting the Gentiles whether they liked it or not so after they'd come to terms with it the Jews puffed out their chests and basically began telling the newbies, *"well we don't like it but if you Gentiles are going to start worshipping our God you're going to need us to show you how we do things around here. You're going to need to be circumcised, celebrate our holidays and festivals, subscribe to our laws on diet and clothing..."* Essentially they were trying to impose the old Law of Moses on the Gentiles and make them culturally Jewish.

The people that tried to do this are known as Judaisers.

The Gentiles were confused. When they heard the gospel for the first time from the likes of Peter and Paul they were told that all they needed to do was put their faith in Jesus for salvation and that would be enough. And so they did. And God confirmed to them that it was enough because He gave them His Holy Spirit and performed signs and wonders amongst them as soon as they believed. But now here were these groups of Jews saying that actually faith alone wasn't enough. That they needed to add the old Jewish rituals and traditions and laws and works too.

This whole issue created such a stir that the apostles formed a council to discuss the issue. This meeting is recorded in the Book of Acts, chapter 15:

"...some of the men who had been Pharisees before their conversion stood up and declared that all Gentile converts must be circumcised and be required to follow the law of Moses. So

the apostles and church elders got together to decide this question. At the meeting, after a long discussion, Peter stood and addressed them as follows: 'Brothers, you all know that God chose me from among you some time ago to preach to the Gentiles so that they could hear the Good News and believe. God, who knows people's hearts, confirmed that he accepted the Gentiles by giving them the Holy Spirit, just as he gave him to us. He made no distinction between us and them, for he also cleansed their hearts through faith. Why are you now questioning God's way by burdening the Gentile believers with a yoke that neither we nor our ancestors were able to bear? We believe that we are all saved the same way, by the special favour of the Lord Jesus." (Acts 15:5-11)

So Peter effectively said, *"look, the old Law of Moses was a burden that none of us have been able to bear. None of our ancestors could bear it either. All it led to was pride, legalism, hypocrisy, bondage and death. So why are you trying to resurrect it and lay that burden on the Gentiles? Why are you trying to bring Judaism into Christianity when the new Spirit-filled life under Christ is so much better than the old? Let the Law of Moses go! We're all saved the same way - by simple faith in what Jesus did for us on the cross."*

You'll be unsurprised to hear it was the legalistic Pharisees that had the hardest time letting go of the Law of Moses and unfortunately, Peter's words didn't deter them. Legalists are never easily deterred. Derek Prince says, *"Legalism has a great hold on the human mind: it appeals to our human pride. That is why people can be passionately dedicated to a legalistic religion."*

These guys were so passionately dedicated to their legalism that they started secretly following the apostles on their missionary journeys around Asia and Europe. The apostles would go from town to town, preaching the true gospel, planting new churches, and then once they had left and gone on to the next town, the Judaisers would sneak in behind them to confuse and pervert the message.

Paul knew what they were doing and said to the elders in Ephesus, *"I know that false teachers, like vicious wolves, will come in among you after I leave, not sparing the flock. Even some men from your own group will rise up and distort the truth to draw a following."* (Acts 20:29-30)

The most famous example of Judaisers coming in after Paul had visited an area was in Galatia. After Paul had been and gone from that region, Judaisers came in and began trying to discredit him. They told the Galatians that Paul wasn't even a real apostle and not to be trusted. They told them that he hadn't given them the whole story. They said that faith in Jesus was good but that they had to add to it the Law of Moses. Unfortunately many of the Galatians started to listen to this pollution. So Paul wrote a letter to the Galatians, at first establishing his credentials as an apostle, and then pleading with them not listen to the false teaching of the Judaisers.

He wrote, *"...some so-called Christians...false ones really...came to spy on us and see our freedom in Christ Jesus. They wanted to force us, like slaves to follow their Jewish regulations. But we refused to listen to them for a single moment. We wanted to preserve the truth of the Good News for you."* (Gal 2:4-5)

Later Paul writes, *"We have believed in Christ Jesus, that we might be accepted by God because of our faith in Christ - and* not because we have obeyed the law. For no one will ever be saved by obeying the law." (2:16) In fact he says, "I make myself guilty if I rebuild the old system I already tore down." (Gal 2:18).

Getting exasperated he exclaims, "Have you lost your senses? After starting your Christian lives in the Spirit why are you now trying to become perfect by your own human effort?" (3:3)

He goes on, "those who depend on the law to make them right with God are under his curse, for the Scriptures say, 'Cursed is everyone who does not observe and obey all these commands that are written in God's Book of the Law.'" (3:10) "If you wish to find life by obeying the law you must obey all of its commands." (3:12) Here Paul tells them that if they try to stay right with God by keeping the law then they have to obey all 613 of them perfectly. And because they'll never be able to do it, they'll just put themselves under the curse of death like the Israelites of old. David Pawson writes, "if we tell people to keep the Law of Moses we are consigning them to hell because they cannot do it."

Paul continues in his letter to the Galatians saying, "Christ has rescued us from the curse pronounced by the law. When he hung on the cross, he took upon himself the curse for our wrongdoing." (4:13)

Getting even more exasperated he writes, "You are trying to find favour with God by what you do or what you don't do on certain days or months or seasons or years. I fear for you. I am afraid that all my hard work for you was worth nothing. Dear brothers and sisters, I plead with you to live as I do in freedom from these things, for I have become like you Gentiles were – free from the law." (Gal 4:10-12).

He goes on to say, *"So Christ has truly set us free. Now make sure that you stay free, and don't get tied up again in slavery to the law."*(5:1) And then he repeats the Law of Christ saying, *"what is important is faith expressing itself in love."* (5:6) and *"the whole law can be summed up in this one command: 'Love your neighbour as yourself.'"*(5:14)

You can hear the emotion building throughout Paul's letter as he pleads with them not to go back to the old system with its oppressive list of rules that lead to death. He wants them just to accept Jesus' sacrifice for them by faith and then love God and one another with all their heart, mind, soul and strength. That is the freedom that they were rejecting by listening to these Judaisers.

And that's the freedom we reject if we try to add the old Law of Moses to the Christian life today.

Before finishing this chapter, I want to say clearly that if you want to become a Christian you don't have to become culturally Jewish. Part of the beauty of the freedom of Christianity is the diversity which it allows for. Because God looks at internal motives over external actions, we have true freedom in worship. So the way Africans worship God is very different to the way Asians worship God and that's very different to the way Europeans and Americans worship God. The instruments are different, the clothes are different, the hairstyles are different. All of it's great. Christianity doesn't demand an imposition of a culture on anyone. The new earth is going to be a colourful place when we get there. People from every tribe, tongue and language. And it will be all the better for it.

I'll cut this chapter short and simply ask you to go read Galatians now because it will give you real insight into this issue. In the light of what you've learned so far, let Paul's words come alive and soak into your mind and heart. In fact, read it more than once.

FURTHER READING: Galatians

SECTION 3
The Truth Will Set You Free

"It is impossible to enslave mentally or socially a Bible-reading people. The principles of the Bible are the groundwork of human freedom."

Horace Greeley

"Outside of the resurrection of Christ I know of no other hope for mankind."

Conrad Adenauer

CHAPTER 14
LEGALISM TODAY

Specifically trying to resurrect the Old Testament Law of Moses to impose it on Christians is called Judaising, but more generally, legalism just means trying to create man-made rights and wrongs on any neutral issues and trying to regulate behaviour through law.

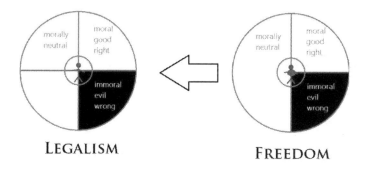

LEGALISM   FREEDOM

It means trying to rebuild a bar over the neutral realm that Christ actually tore down.

So legalism is actually far more extensive than Judaising. The Law of Moses had only 613 rules but the amount of legalistic rules that people can come up with for neutral issues are actually endless. Don't drink that. Don't eat that. Don't wear that. (Col 2:21) Remember, it's to the legalists that Jesus said, *"Their worship is a farce, and they teach man-made ideas as commands from God."* (Matt 15:9)

Here are some prominent examples of legalism that may be found in churches today.

Legalism in Worship

Clothes

It's quite common for Christians to be legalistic about clothes in church. Some people say that jeans should not be worn in church. Some say that suits are the only acceptable apparel for worship. Some insist that women wear hats. And that the pastor wears a tie. Clothes are morally neutral and Jesus says nothing about them so when we apply the Law of Christ we discover that actually we have freedom in this. All that matters is the motivation.

So if a guy who wears a suit does so because he wants to show God his love and respect by wearing his best clothes, then he is following the Law of Christ and that's great. But equally, if the guy who wears jeans is doing it because he feels he can give God more focus if he's comfortable with what he's wearing, then he's following the Law of Christ too. And that's equally great. The external action - how their love presents itself outwardly - is different, but their motivation is actually the same. So both are equally right. It's legalism to insist that people must wear certain items of clothing.

Music

It's equally common for people to be legalistic about music too. Some complain that drums or guitars are inappropriate for church. The older generations may insist that organs or pianos are the only acceptable instruments for worship.

Music instruments are morally neutral items. They are not inherently sinful. It's through tradition more than anything that some people have decided that some of them are.

So we are actually free to use any of them and all of them to worship God. Psalm 150 tells people to praise him with the horn, the lyre, the harp, the tambourine, with dancing, with strings and flutes and with the clash of loud clanging cymbals. In other words, whatever you can lay your hands on!

We all have musical preferences but it's idolatrous legalism to insist that what you prefer is what God would prefer too. Don't create God in your own image. It's ok if you prefer the sound of a piano to a guitar but it's equally ok if someone else likes the reverse. Again, this is often a generational thing so young people, don't look down on older people for their preferences. Old people, don't look down on younger people for theirs. Let each person worship God in a way that is meaningful.

Emotion

Similarly, I've heard people talk disapprovingly of those who are showing too much excitement or emotion in church because they feel people should be reverent and sombre...just like they are.

There is room for everything. And there is a time for everything.

If you are happy in God then express it with joy. If you are feeling pain then cry on His shoulder. If you are suddenly aware of His holiness then stand in reverence and awe. Just be authentic with your worship. Be spontaneous. Be extravagant.

Remember when King David felt so blessed by God that he felt the urge to dance? So that's exactly what he did! He was dancing so hard that the garment he was wearing failed to preserve his modesty and he exposed himself to onlookers. When his wife saw him she was angry and said sarcastically, *"How distinguished the king of Israel looked today shamelessly exposing himself to the servant girls like any vulgar person might do!"* David replied with no shame at all saying, *"I was dancing before the Lord...He appointed me as the leader of Israel, the people of the Lord, so I celebrate before the Lord. Yes, and I am willing to look even more foolish than this, even to be humiliated in my own eyes!"* (2 Sam 6:20-22).

David isn't thinking of how he looks at all. He's so caught up in God that thoughts of himself have disappeared. He's thinking of God first and himself last - fulfilling the Law of Christ. That is the freedom we have too. Forget tradition, the way it's always been done, forget who is around you, forget how foolish you might look and just be authentic with God. Love him freely. Church is a place for dancing and celebration as well as reverence and fear.

Sunday

Some people are legalistic with Sunday saying that you shouldn't lift a finger that day. They say that it's a sin to play sport or even go for a walk. Because that's work.

Sunday is a neutral day. So enjoy your freedom in Christ! Enjoy His creation and His goodness. Go for a walk, relax, play sport. Shake off the legalism! Jesus famously told the Pharisees, *"The Sabbath was made to meet the needs of people, and not people to meet the requirements of the Sabbath."* (Mark 2:27) In other words, the principle of taking a day off in the week to recharge is meant to be for your benefit; it's not meant to exist as a burdensome law that you exist to fulfil. Do what helps you recharge and do it with God's blessing.

In the movie, Chariots of Fire, the true story of Eric Lidell is told. He wouldn't run on a Sunday because his conscience told him not to and he was blessed for obeying that conscience. He was putting God first. But if his conscience hadn't bothered him then he could just as easily have run on Sunday and God would have blessed that too! That's the freedom of Christ's law. Simply react to your conscience and the leading of the Holy Spirit.

"The world doesn't need my tie, my hoodie, my denomination, or my translation of the Bible. They just need Jesus." - Mark Hall

LEGALISM IN THE SABBATH

And that leads us onto a wider issue concerning the Sabbath.

The Sabbath under the Law of Moses was actually a Saturday rather than a Sunday and there are certain Judaisers out there, most notably the Seventh Day Adventists, who say we should go back to a Saturday Sabbath in keeping with the Law of Moses. And that to worship on any other day is a sin.

Nonsense.

The Law of Moses is gone. Days are morally neutral. Therefore, you are free to worship God on any day you like.

The early church were so driven by love that they actually met *every* day of the week. In Acts 2:46 it says, *"They worshipped together at the Temple every day, met in homes for the Lord's Supper, and shared their meals with great joy and generosity."* They wanted to hang out together as often as they could and share generously their time and food with one another. See the mindset change again? They were no longer thinking about fulfilling a minimum requirement or a law. They were not asking what they could get away with. They were using their freedom in Christ to be extravagant, authentic and spontaneous with their love for one another! Love has no limits and boundaries. They didn't *have* to meet every day, there were no rules on such things, no liturgy, but because they loved each other they *wanted* to!

Now it's true that Acts still records the apostles going to the synagogue on Saturday but it appears to mainly be because they knew that's where the crowds would be on that day and it would be a good chance to evangelise. Acts 17:2 says, *"As was Paul's custom, he went to the synagogue service, and for three Sabbaths in a row he used the scriptures to reason with the people."* This is what Paul did. He worked out where the crowds would be then he went there with the gospel. On a Saturday Sabbath the synagogue is where the Jewish crowds would be so that's where he went. Paul explains this evangelism technique later on saying, *"When I was with the Jews, I lived like a Jew to bring the Jews to Christ...Even though I am not subject to the law, I did this so I could bring to Christ those who are under the law."* (1 Cor 9:20) Paul wasn't going to the synagogue on the Sabbath because he felt constrained by the Sabbath law. He was going to the synagogue on the Sabbath to help those in bondage to the law be *free* of it!

Adventists and other legalists will often try to frame this debate in Saturday v Sunday terms believing that those who go to church on Sunday have been perverted and deceived by a subversive edict from the Roman Emperor Constantine. This is a false framework for the argument that shows a complete lack of understanding of the freedom we now have in Christ. The truth is that while Christians generally do have their main worship gatherings on Sunday, we could just as easily worship on Monday, Tuesday, Wednesday, Thursday, Friday or Saturday and as long as we were doing it with the right motivation, each day would all be perfectly acceptable to God. We're not enslaved to Sunday any more than we're enslaved to Saturday. We can, and should, worship any day, either day, all day, every day. We are free from *all* rules on such things. Just do what you do as unto the Lord, with the right heart. That's all. To prove the point, it should be noted that the apostles did also explicitly meet on a Sunday themselves, as recorded in 1 Cor 16:1-2 and Acts 20:7. Constantine's role is actually almost irrelevant.

There is no truth to the fanciful claim that by meeting on a Sunday Christians are automatically worshipping the pagan sun god. Any more than worshipping on a Saturday would cause us to be worshipping Saturn or worshipping on Thursday would cause us to be worshipping Thor, after whom those days are named. Forgive me for being repetitive but the truth is, if you want to love God by meeting on a Saturday, then do it. If you want to do it by meeting on a Sunday, then do that. If you want to do it every day, then all the better. With regard to neutral issues like clothes, holidays and Sabbaths, what matters is your motivation; God looks at your heart. Don't be legalistic and set rules about such things. Meet as often as possible! And share all good things generously with one another. That is the mindset change. That is the freedom to love that you now have.

"No Bible-taught Christian can allow himself to live in bondage to days and times and seasons. He knows he is free from the Law, and the Judaising brethren who seek to rivet a yoke on his neck will not have much success." - A.W. Tozer

HOLIDAYS

Legalism in weekdays leads us onto legalism in holidays.

In *Know Your Enemy* I explained that December 25th is not the real birthday of Jesus but that we use that date because it was when the pagans used to celebrate the birth of the sun god. The church in Rome just came along and said, *"well, we're never going to get people to give up that date - it's too embedded in culture - so let's just keep the date and celebrate Christ's birth then."* I also explained that the word 'Easter' comes from 'Ishtar', which is the Celtic form of the Babylonian fertility goddess, Ashteroth/Asherah. And that the secular elements of the Easter celebration are also rooted in paganism - things like bunnies and eggs.

I then went on to say that even though all this was true, Christians were in fact free to celebrate Jesus' birth on 25th December if they wanted and they were free to celebrate His death and resurrection every Spring too (although I did suggest we change the name from 'Easter' to something more appropriate). I said it was ok to do this as long as it was done 'as unto the Lord' i.e. with the right heart motivation. I expected retaliation and arguments on many aspects of *Know Your Enemy* but I didn't expect that this would be by far the biggest controversy of the series. *"How can you condone people celebrating Jesus' birth and his death and resurrection on pagan dates?"* people asked.

Well, of course, there's no such thing as a 'pagan date'. All days of the year are morally neutral. Which means they can all be manipulated and used 'as unto the Lord'. And trying to restrict or control the days on which people can worship Jesus is hard-hearted legalism.

So rather than apologise for our freedom in Christ, let me go one step further and say that actually, you can celebrate His coming on any day of the year you like! March 16th, June 9th, November 21st...pick one! In fact, you can celebrate it every single day of the year. And you can certainly celebrate it on 25th December. We are not bound by any laws to any specific days at all and are free to use them to honour and love God in any way we wish.

Please listen to the words of Paul when he says, *"Let no man therefore judge you in meat or drink, or in respect to a holy day or the new moon or the Sabbath days."* (Col 2:16) To the Romans he wrote, *"some think one day is more holy than another day, while others think every day is alike. You should each be fully convinced that whichever day you choose is acceptable. Those who worship the Lord on a special day do it to honour him. Those who eat any kind of food do so to honour the Lord, since they give thanks to God before eating. And those who refuse to eat certain foods also want to please the Lord and give thanks to God." (Rom 14:5-6).* To those in Galatia he wrote, *"why do you want to go back again and become slaves once more to the weak and useless spiritual principles of this world? You are trying to earn favour with God by observing certain days or months or seasons or years." (Gal 4:9)*

Are you doing what you're doing to love and honour God with a clear conscience? Then fine. Go ahead and do it. And let no-one judge you for it. You are following the Law of Christ and you'll be blessed for it. If your conscience bothers you and you don't want to celebrate Jesus' birth in December then pick another day and do it then. That's your freedom. What matters is whether your motivation in using those days is to love and honour God. How that intent expresses itself is really up to you.

Some Complications...

Now I'll admit that celebrating Jesus' birth on December 25th does throw up some complications. For example, what do we do with Santa Claus? Can we honestly say Santa Claus is helpful in our efforts to focus on the birth of Christ? Is he not, in fact, much more of a distraction? Doesn't he take our focus away from Jesus rather than towards him? Doesn't he compete with our affections for Jesus? If so, are we really honouring and loving Jesus the best we can by making Santa a part of our celebrations? Probably not.

Similarly, is there any sense in which the Easter Bunny helps us focus on and honour Christ? Is it not more of a distraction too? A pollutant? Doesn't it take our focus away from Christ? I think so.

Well, if those things are getting in the way of Christ then they need to go. Anything that gets itself in the way of Christ needs to go.

What about the commercialism of modern Christmas celebrations and the stress it brings? Is there any sense in which that brings us closer to Jesus? Aren't we just following the world into consumerism, materialism and greed with those things? If so, then that needs to go too.

You see, although it's permissible for us to celebrate Jesus on these established holidays, we have to still discern what's beneficial. In fact Paul said that very thing. He said, *"everything is permissible - but not everything is beneficial."* (1 Cor 10:23)

We need to do what's beneficial.

To avoid these complications with Santa and suchlike, would it be beneficial to separate our celebrations of Jesus' birth out from the secular idea of Christmas and move it to its real date? Would it be beneficial to celebrate his death and resurrection on its real date too? Quite possibly. It's a radical idea but it's worth thinking about. Maybe to avoid the confusion and the potential for secular pollution we should think about moving our celebrations.

Jesus was actually born on the Jewish Feast of Tabernacles which would place it in September/October each year. His death and resurrection occurred around the Jewish Feast of Passover, which actually isn't that far removed from Easter in Spring. Maybe we would have a clearer focus on Jesus if we moved the celebrations to those dates. If you want to make a personal decision to do that then feel free.

Not only might it help you focus on Christ without the sideshow of Santa and the Easter Bunny but there's a very good case for saying that the Jewish Feasts are prophetic. Therefore, if we connect our present holidays to the feasts, we will come to greater understanding of the present and the future.

If the Holy Spirit prompts you in this way then follow His leading by all means. As a church we should have a discussion about this. But...in the meantime...don't be so irrationally legalistic in neutral issues to insist that others are going to hell for celebrating Christ's birth in December. That's the same kind of nonsensical thinking that saw the Pharisees fighting with each other over how many jugs of milk they could lift on the Sabbath. People are free in Christ to express their love how they choose on any day they choose. What matters is the motive.

Can I also take this opportunity to answer the objection that because Jesus didn't specifically command a holiday for His own birth or resurrection, we shouldn't celebrate the occasions at all. If that is your position, you are holding to the old Judaic mindset of waiting for God to set rules and laws so that you can meet their minimum requirements. You have missed the whole message of the Gospel. Under the Law of Christ, we are to have the new mindset where we proactively think of ways to express our love for God and others spontaneously, authentically and extravagantly. Why wouldn't we want to celebrate the greatest events in history and thank Jesus for His gift of grace? It's a natural expression of love for him. Worship Him freely. Let's not be like the Pharisees and condemn each other for it.

Finally, let me also repeat what I said about Halloween in *Know Your Enemy*. Although 31st October is a neutral day which we can indeed use to honour and love God, the Halloween celebration itself has no reference to Christ at all and is very simply a glorification of evil, fear, darkness, Satan, demons, witches and horror; all of which is the very antithesis of everything Jesus stands for. Therefore there is absolutely no sense in which we can celebrate those things out of love for Christ. It's a complete oxymoron. It's like saying you can honour your wife by sleeping with another woman. Or like saying you can curse or lie or steal unto the Lord. Let's not fool ourselves. If you're dressed up as Satan and think Jesus is ok with that, then something has gone wrong. John Muncee said, *"You'll never be able to speak against evil if you're entertained by it."* I think if we examine our hearts honestly we'll discover the real reason why so many Christians don't want to give up Halloween is because we're simply entertained by evil.

Remember, our freedom is not freedom to do what we want - that's the Law of Satan. Our freedom is rather to love God and others freely by the leading of the Holy Spirit. But please, do enjoy your freedom under the Law of Christ to celebrate His birth and resurrection on any day you wish, and if there are any other days that are meaningful to your walk with the Lord then by all means mark those with celebrations too. Don't let legalists look down on you for it.

TITHING

Another area where legalism is present today in the church is in regards to tithing. Under the old Law of Moses people were instructed to give a strict 10% of their income. But money is a neutral thing and under the Law of Christ we have freedom. So tithing has been replaced with the idea of free, authentic, spontaneous and extravagant giving. Paul writes, *"I want you to excel also in this gracious ministry of giving. I am not saying you must do it, even though the other churches are eager to do it. This is one way to prove your love is real."* (2 Cor 8:8) So you don't *have* to give - you're under no compulsion - but if you truly love others then surely you'll *want* to give! Giving is a natural consequence of love.

He then says, *"You must each make up your own mind as to how much you should give. Don't give reluctantly or in response to pressure. For God loves the person who gives cheerfully."* (2 Cor 9:7) There's no set amounts on how much you have to give. No rules. No laws. No percentages. No minimum requirements. Just give whatever you think you can out of love and do it with a smile on your face! When a parent gives a child a present do they do it grudgingly? Of course not! Why not? Because it gives them great joy to be able to bless their children with a gift because they love them. We should have that same attitude towards each other. Be happy to share what you have!

Jesus said, *"it is more blessed to give than to receive."* (Acts 20:35) He also says, *"Give, and you will receive. Your gift will return to you in full—pressed down, shaken together to make room for more, running over, and poured into your lap. The amount you give will determine the amount you get back." (Luke 6:38)* He's not just speaking in a monetary sense there. The principle is universal. Love generates love. The more you give love away the more you get in return. That's why a society living by the Law of Christ becomes such a great place to be. Love is generating love in others and so it multiplies and comes back to you.

If you haven't done the gift giving experiment with your wife or girlfriend yet, do it now and watch this principle in action. Because you're more free with your love they'll be more free with theirs. I hope I'm managing to communicate that the Law of Christ is never an excuse to give less; it's an excuse to give more. It's an excuse to give freely and extravagantly and spontaneously.

Indeed, love freely gives twice as much as duty can demand.

Legalism In Other Religions

One final example of religious legalism...but this time not in Christianity...we're going to look at legalism in other religions.

Because every single religion in the world is legalistic.

Christianity is unique in offering freedom from legalism and salvation by faith alone.

The fundamental idea behind all world religions is, *"do this, this and this...follow these laws...and if you do enough good things and follow all the rules well enough, that might earn you a path into heaven."*

So for example, in Islam, you *have* to pray 5 times a day to stay right with Allah. In contrast Christians have no set times and can pray spontaneously and authentically as often as they like. Muslims can *only* eat halal meat. Christians can eat anything with a clear conscience and thanksgiving. Muslims *must* fast during the month of Ramadan. Christians can fast as often as they like, as the Spirit moves them or as the situation requires. Islam says you *have* to make a pilgrimage to Mecca. Christianity has no such rule, although our love of Jesus makes us intrigued to see where He lived and preached.

Religious legalism burdens people with lists of minimum requirements designed to make yourself acceptable to God. Freedom under the Law of Christ says your good works can't make God love you any more or any less than He already does. He already loves you so much that He died on a cross for you. All that's left for you to do in is love him authentically, spontaneously and extravagantly in return. And that's one of the key differences between Christianity and every other faith system in the world.

When Afghanistan was ruled by the Islamic Taliban regime, the legalism said that no one in the country was allowed to sing or dance, music was banned, people were not allowed to own photographs of living things, and they were not allowed to play sports. In Somalia today, the national football team have to play their matches in secret because the Muslim group al-Shabab threaten the lives of those who play the game, believing it to be a tool of the devil. They won't even tolerate it being watched on TV. That's a few examples of the heavy oppression of religious legalism and you'll find it in all religions to some extent. Only through Christ are people freed from such thinking.

This is why we Christians sometimes object to Christianity being labelled a 'religion' at all, and insist on calling it a 'relationship' with God instead. Although it's strictly true to call Christianity a religion in the sense that it answers the big questions of life, the word has baggage which evokes ideas of legalistic rules, rituals and minimum requirements...because that's what all other religions are all about. That's not Christianity though. Christians prefer the term 'relationship' to describe our faith because it evokes a more accurate sense of free interaction with God via the Holy Spirit.

This also explains why we Christians don't believe in mantras, vain repetition, dead ritual, liturgy and set prayer books. Saying endless "Hail Mary's" in an attempt to absolve sins has no use for us. Do you speak to your friends or any other sentient beings by repeating the same words endlessly? No? Then why a living God? Jesus said, *"When you pray, don't babble on and on as people of other religions do. They think their prayers are answered merely by repeating their words again and again. Don't be like them..."* (Matt 6:7) We're after truth, authenticity, deep relationship and spontaneous worship. We want to engage with God as the living being that He is.

John Eldredge wrote, *"There are no formulas with God. Period. So there are no formulas for a man who follows him. God is a Person, not a doctrine. He operates not like a system - not even a theological system - but with all the originality of a truly free and alive person."*

Do you feel how easy and light Jesus' yoke is yet? Do you see how little He burdens you? Am I managing to communicate this to you? Do you feel the oppressive weight of the law coming off your shoulders here? Jesus doesn't force you to meet mountains of rules. He gives you freedom and then says, "use it to love others like I love you." (Matt 10:8)

Augustine summed up the Christian life very succinctly when he said, "Love God and then do what you want." Because if you truly love God above everything else, if he is first in your life, then what you want will primarily be to honour him. And when honouring God is your primary thought, everything else takes care of itself. You will automatically fulfil the eternal MORAL LAW and you will use neutral things for His glory. Indeed, everything you think, say and do will automatically start to align with God's will and as you follow the leading of the Holy Spirit, your conscience will be sharpened, your desires will change, and you will start to be transformed into a new person. All this will happen without any need for excessive rules or ritual and the change will be lasting because it will be internal. God will place a new, responsive and tender heart in his followers by His Spirit. And we are indeed called to live under the Spirit, not under the law. Stay free! Love God and then do what you want.

"He has enabled us to be ministers of his new covenant. This is a covenant not of written laws, but of the Spirit. The old written covenant ends in death; but under the new covenant, the Spirit brings life." (2 Cor 3:6)

CHAPTER 15
PAUL'S LETTER ON LEGALISM

I'll now let Paul have the final word on legalism. This is what he said to the Christians in Rome:

"Accept other believers who are weak in faith, and don't argue with them about what they think is right or wrong. For instance, one person believes it's all right to eat anything. But another believer with a sensitive conscience will eat only vegetables. Those who feel free to eat anything must not look down on those who don't. And those who don't eat certain foods must not condemn those who do, for God has accepted them. Who are you to condemn someone else's servants? Their own master will judge whether they stand or fall. And with the Lord's help, they will stand and receive his approval.

In the same way, some think one day is more holy than another day, while others think every day is alike. You should each be fully convinced that whichever day you choose is acceptable. Those who worship the Lord on a special day do it to honour him. Those who eat any kind of food do so to honour the Lord, since they give thanks to God before eating. And those who refuse to eat certain foods also want to please the Lord and give thanks to God. For we don't live for ourselves or die for ourselves. If we live, it's to honour the Lord. And if we die, it's to honour the Lord. So whether we live or die, we belong to the Lord. Christ died and rose again for this very purpose—to be Lord both of the living and of the dead.

So why do you condemn another believer? Why do you look down on another believer? Remember, we will all stand before the judgment seat of God. For the Scriptures say,

"'As surely as I live,' says the LORD,
'every knee will bend to me,
and every tongue will confess and give praise to God.'"

Yes, each of us will give a personal account to God. So let's stop condemning each other. Decide instead to live in such a way that you will not cause another believer to stumble and fall.

I know and am convinced on the authority of the Lord Jesus that no food, in and of itself, is wrong to eat. But if someone believes it is wrong, then for that person it is wrong. And if another believer is distressed by what you eat, you are not acting in love if you eat it. Don't let your eating ruin someone for whom Christ died. Then you will not be criticized for doing something you believe is good. For the Kingdom of God is not a matter of what we eat or drink, but of living a life of goodness and peace and joy in the Holy Spirit. If you serve Christ with this attitude, you will please God, and others will approve of you, too. So then, let us aim for harmony in the church and try to build each other up.

Don't tear apart the work of God over what you eat. Remember, all foods are acceptable, but it is wrong to eat something if it makes another person stumble. It is better not to eat meat or drink wine or do anything else if it might cause another believer to stumble. You may believe there's nothing wrong with what you are doing, but keep it between yourself and God. Blessed are those who don't feel guilty for doing something they have decided is right. But if you have doubts about whether or not you should eat something, you are sinning if you go ahead and

do it. For you are not following your convictions [or conscience].
If you do anything you believe is not right, you are sinning."

We may know these things make no difference, but we cannot
just go ahead and do them to please ourselves. We must be
considerate of the doubts and fears of those who think these
things are wrong. We should please others. If we do what helps
them, we will build them up in the Lord. For even Christ didn't
live to please himself."

(Romans 14, 15:1-3)

Put your faith in Christ for salvation, love God and others before
yourself, always go with your conscience, and don't cause
others to sin by making them go against theirs. Remember their
needs come first. Follow this and you'll fulfil the Law of Christ.

Chapter 16
Between Two Pits

This is where I hope the symbolic language throughout this book has been making sense because we're now going to bring it all together.

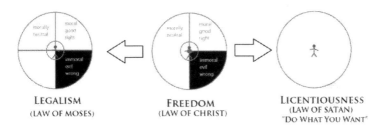

LEGALISM	FREEDOM	LICENTIOUSNESS
(LAW OF MOSES)	(LAW OF CHRIST)	(LAW OF SATAN) "DO WHAT YOU WANT"

On the one side we have explored **legalism**, which is basically burdening people with oppressive rules in a bid to regulate their behaviour - the mistake of the Pharisees under The Law of Moses. The mistake of 'religion' in general. The mistake which doesn't realise that law has no power to change hearts.

The polar opposite to the error of legalism is the error of **licentiousness**. That's when people throw out God altogether, thereby losing their moral reference point, breaking their moral compass, their sense of right and wrong, and where people end up just doing whatever they want. They become their own gods and inevitably follow their own sinful hearts to indulgence and self-destruction.

In the middle we have true **freedom** or **liberty**. The way announced by Jesus Christ were rules are minimal, people are free, but they use their freedom to *choose* good because they have the Holy Spirit within their hearts, regenerating them, giving them new desires and a new nature.

True freedom only exists in this middle way.

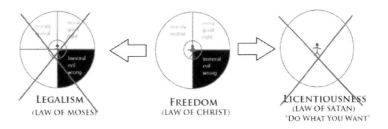

Legalism leads to mountains of burdensome laws that crush people and which takes away their freedom to make their own decisions. They're coerced and forced and regulated into behaving the 'right way' and actually it doesn't even work because it doesn't change hearts desires.

Licentiousness means becoming a slave to sin. Our moral compasses break and the sinful nature within starts to pull us towards selfish indulgence and gratification. And that leads to disease, impotence, jealousy, self-destruction and death.

For true freedom, we need the Holy Spirit within us, regenerating our hearts, giving us new desires and a new nature. It's only by taking the middle road that we can not only *know* what the MORAL LAW is, but we have gain a desire to choose the MORAL LAW. The Spirit heals our heart sickness.

If the symbol language isn't working for you, this one might explain it better:

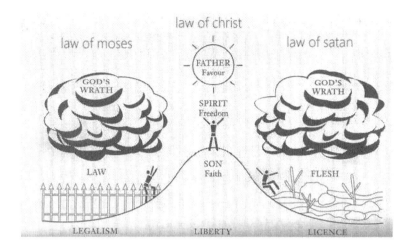

This image shows us that we have true freedom through the middle path, with two equal but opposite pits of error either side of us.

CS Lewis wrote, "*[The Devil] always sends errors into the world in pairs - pairs of opposites. And he always encourages us to spend a lot of time thinking which is the worse. You see why, of course? He relies on your extra dislike of one error to draw you gradually into the opposite one. But do not let us be fooled. We have to keep our eyes on the goal and go straight through between both errors. We have no other concern than that with either of them.*" (Mere Christianity)

We're now going to spend a little bit of time exploring how it is that when we leave one pit, we can often just end up falling into the other.

CHAPTER 17
FROM LEGALISM TO LICENCE

Back when people first discovered they were being set free from the Law of Moses, their first reaction was something like this:

"You mean we're free from the Law of Moses? Does that mean there's no law at all now? Do we live under lawlessness now? Can we just go and do what we want?"

They were about to swap the pit of legalism for the pit of licentiousness. Paul addressed that mindset in Romans 6 by asking the rhetorical question, *"So since God's grace has set us free from the law, does this mean we can go on sinning?"* (Rom 6:15) In other words, "can we just do what we want now?" Then he answers himself saying, *"Of course not! Don't you realise that whatever you choose to obey becomes your master? You can choose sin, which leads to death, or you can choose to obey God and receive his approval."* (Rom 6:15-16)

Paul is saying that once we have established our freedom from the law we can now choose to use that freedom in two ways. You can follow the Law of Christ which leads to freedom or you can follow the Law of Satan by using your freedom to indulge the sinful nature and end up in the equal but opposite pit of licentiousness. And he says that in choosing your path, you will have two opposite forces fighting for supremacy in your heart.

Paul says, *"the [Holy] spirit gives us desires that are opposite from what the sinful nature desires. These two forces are constantly fighting each other and your choices are never free from this conflict." (Galatians 5:17)*

Our inherent sinful nature will tell us to go the path of self-indulgence and greed while the Holy Spirit living within pulls us towards the Law of Christ. Towards selfless love of God and others. Jesus called these two paths the broad road that leads to hell and the narrow road that leads to eternal life. Paul urges Christians to choose the right path with their freedom saying, *"you have been called to live in freedom – not freedom to satisfy your sinful nature, but freedom to serve one another in love." (Gal 5:13)*

Yes, you have freedom from the law. But how will you use it? Your actions will prove whose kingdom you actually belong to - Jesus' or Satan's. Your actions will tell the world whether your heart is currently subject to entropy (a sign that the sinful nature is still in control) or sanctification (a sign that the Holy Spirit has entered in and has taken control).

If you are genuinely following the Spirit you will be sanctified and the fruits of the Spirit will become evident: *"love, joy, peace, patience, kindness, goodness, faithfulness, gentleness and self-control." (Gal 5:22-23)*

However, if the Holy Spirit isn't at work, you will experience heart entropy as the sinful nature runs its course. Paul says, *"When you follow the desires of your sinful nature, your lives will produce these evil results: sexual immorality, impure thoughts, eagerness for lustful pleasure, idolatry, participation in demonic activities, hostility, quarrelling, jealousy, outbursts of anger, selfish ambition, divisions, the feeling that everyone is wrong except those in your own little group, envy, drunkenness, wild parties and other kinds of sin. Let me tell you again, as I have before, that anyone living that sort of life will not inherit the Kingdom of God."* (Gal 5:19-21)

Anyone who chooses the latter path will not inherit the kingdom of God. Paul says, *"But He will pour out his anger an wrath on those who live for themselves."* (Rom 2:8)

This is pertinent stuff because even within churches we can find people living for themselves and showing no signs of sanctification. We can often find people claiming freedom from the law but seeming to think that gives them licence to sin. We can often find self-proclaimed Christians coming out of the pit of legalism but shooting right past true freedom and into the opposite pit of licentiousness. That is, 'doing whatever we want' i.e. following our sinful nature. And thinking God is fine with it.

Therefore, it's not uncommon to see people claim a faith in Christ, go to church on Sunday, but yet live their lives licentiously. Sleeping around, partying as hard as the rest, littering their speech with blasphemies and swearing, being entertained by wickedness and basically follow their sinful natures at every turn.

Randy Alcorn rightly says, *"Any concept of grace that makes us feel more comfortable sinning is not biblical grace. God's grace never encourages us to live in sin, on the contrary, it empowers us to say no to sin and yes to truth."*

Peter said, *"You are not slaves; you are free. But your freedom is not an excuse to do evil."* (1 Peter 2:16)

AW Tozer writes, *"The idea that God will pardon a rebel who has not given up his rebellion is contrary both to the Scriptures and to common sense."*

The freedom from the law that Christ offers is not freedom to sin; it's freedom *not* to sin. It's freedom *not* to be enslaved by our sinful desires. It's freedom to live by the Spirit. To be given new natures and new hearts.

The Bible is pretty clear about this: If your life doesn't eventually start to reflect what you claim to believe, the truth is, you don't really believe it. If you're not being sanctified by the Spirit, you don't really have the Spirit within you. You're not really following Jesus. You're actually following Satan. You're actually following his "do what you want" golden rule. And you won't inherit the kingdom of God that way. Those who live by the Spirit will do what the Spirit says.

Jesus said, *"So why do you keep calling me 'Lord, Lord!' when you don't do what I say?" (Luke 6:46)*

He's not your Lord if you're not obedient to him. And if he's not your Lord, he's not your Saviour either.

John said, *"And how can we be sure we belong to him? By obeying his commandments. If someone says, "I belong to God," but doesn't obey God's commandments, that person is a liar and does not live in the truth." - 1 John 2:3-4*

What is Jesus' commandment? What is the Law of Christ? Jesus said, *"This is my commandment: Love each other in the same way I have loved you." (John 15:9-12)*

Your actions speak louder than your words. True faith will show in your actions. In coming out of the pit of legalism and celebrating your freedom from the law, be very careful how you use that freedom. It's not freedom to sin. Be very careful not to jump right into the other pit of licentiousness.

Charles Spurgeon wrote, *"If you have been truly born again you have a new and holy nature, and you are no longer moved towards sinful objects as you were before. The things that you once loved you now hate, and therefore you will not run after them. You can hardly understand it but so it is, that your thoughts and tastes are radically changed. You long for that very holiness which once it was irksome to hear of; and you loathe those vain pursuits which were once your delights. The man who puts his trust in the Lord sees the pleasures of sin in a new light. For he sees the evil which follows them by noting the agonies which they brought upon our Lord when He bore our sins in His own body on the tree."*

All Spurgeon is really saying here is that if the Spirit is really within you, you're going to have a new heart. You're going to want to use your freedom to love God and others before yourself and you'll want to fulfil the Law of Christ. True faith, true heart regeneration, will show.

TRUE FAITH SHOWS

The Bible has so much to say on this topic. Jesus compared true heart regeneration to fruit blossoming on a tree saying, *"Yes, just as you can identify a tree by its fruits, so you can identify people by their actions."* (Matt 7:20)

Just as good fruit is a natural and visible sign of a good tree, good external actions are a natural and visible sign of a healthy, regenerated, sanctified, Spirit-controlled heart. If someone claims they're a good tree but aren't producing good fruit, they're only fooling themselves and they don't really have the Spirit within them.

James wrote a lot on the issue of how genuine love of God would show in our actions. He said, *"if you just listen but don't obey, you are only fooling yourself."* (James 1:22)

He said, *"If you claim to be religious but don't control your tongue, you are just fooling yourself and your religion is worthless. Pure and lasting religion in the sight of God our Father means we must care for orphans and widows in their troubles and refuse to let the world corrupt us."* (1:26)

True faith shows.

He then says, *"Faith that doesn't show itself by good deeds is no faith at all - it is dead and useless. Now someone may argue, 'some people have faith; others have good deeds.' I say, 'I can't see your faith if you don't have good deeds, but I will show you my faith through my good deeds.' Do you still think it's enough just to believe that there is one God? Well, even the demons believe this, and they tremble in terror! Fool! When will you ever learn that faith that does not result in good deeds is useless?"* (2:17-20)

Dietrich Bonhoeffer put it very succinctly when he said, *"Only the believing obey, only the obedient believe."* If you don't obey Jesus through the leading of the Spirit, then despite what your lips say, you don't really believe. You're still just following your own selfish nature. You have not truly been born again.

True faith shows!

By faith Noah built an ark; by faith Abraham lived in tents all his life; by faith Moses left the comfort of Egypt to take Israel through the desert; by faith Israel marched round Jericho at the command of God; by faith Gideon, Barak, Samson, Jephthah,

David, Samuel, John the Baptist, Peter, Paul and all the prophets and apostles overthrew kingdoms, ruled with justice, shut the mouths of lions, quenched the flames of fire, put armies to flight, healed the sick, cast out demons and raised the dead. (Heb 11) Look through the Bible and you'll discover that wherever there is great faith there is always great accompanying action. True faith *always* translates into action. It always reveals itself in what we say and do.

If your idea of Christianity is attending services and claiming you believe in God but then living according to your own sinful desires, you've missed the point. You're in the pit of licentiousness.

DON'T GET DESPONDENT

Now I don't want people to get despondent here as they look at their own imperfections. It's important to realise that in some cases the struggle between self and the Spirit may go on for months or years or decades or whole lifetimes. From this day until the day you die you're going to keep sinning. Sanctification doesn't happen in an instant and you're going to fall down a lot. And be sure that doesn't cut you off from Christ.

But if you're genuinely living by the Spirit, sanctification will happen. You will get better. You will win some inner battles. And you'll want to keep fighting those battles. That desire to keep fighting with them is a good sign because it shows you're on the right track. It's when you stop struggling, stop caring, your conscience falls silent and you start revelling in your sin that it's time to worry.

It's also important to realise that we all have different starting points and different battles to fight so we should be very slow to judge another person's walk. Someone who struggles with sexual addiction may not struggle at all with alcohol addiction. Another who struggles with alcohol addiction may not struggle at all with sexual addiction. They should be slow to judge one another for falling down in battles that they've never had to fight personally. And anyone who is fighting battles and losing some is doing better than someone who isn't fighting at all. Slow sanctification is sanctification still and is always better than entropy.

We should never discourage anyone who is making progress, no matter how slowly. Indeed, we should help one another on our journeys.

LEGALISM BREEDS LICENCE

Finally, it's important to note that religious legalism actually *causes* people to become licentious. It repels them into licentiousness.

You see, when children grow up under churchy legalism, it feels suffocating and oppressive. Remember how Jesus berated the Pharisees saying, *"you crush people with unbearable religious demands, and you never lift a finger to ease the burden." (Luke 11:46)?* Mountains of laws are crushing and children who grow up under religious legalism know this better than anyone.

Remember how legalism tended to lead to cold-heartedness too? Well children growing up under religious legalism suffer the most from that cold-heartedness.

And remember how legalism tended to cause people to become hypocritical too? Like whitewashed tombs? Well, people growing up under religious legalism tend to see that hypocrisy at close quarters too.

As those children grow up under those conditions, they naturally come to despise the hypocrisy, cold heartedness and suffocating rules that they knew, and when that legalism was imposed in the name of Christianity, they come to despise God as the root of their suffering.

In this moment, "do what you want" living sounds particularly tempting. It sounds like freedom from legalism. So when the child is old enough to make their own decisions, they will run as far away from legalism as they can possibly get, they'll shoot right past freedom and they'll end up in the pit of licence.

When they've been brought up being told, thou shalt do anything on a Sunday, thou shalt not watch TV, thou shalt not play sports, thou shalt not drink alcohol, thou shalt not date etc. as soon as they're old enough, they'll rebel against it all. They'll "do what they want". They'll experiment with sex, drugs, alcohol and anything else that subverts and breaks the rules they grew up with.

Some of the most ardent and vitriolic atheists that you'll ever meet are people who were raised under religious legalism. They're now in the other pit, enslaved to sin, following the Law of Satan, and with their moral compasses broken, will soon find themselves heading towards disease, jealousy, pain and death.

CHAPTER 18
FROM LICENCE TO LEGALISM

Not only can legalism drive people into licence, but the reverse can happen too.

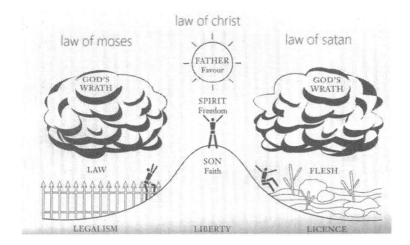

Here are some scenarios that might sound familiar:

- Society is becoming damaged by a licentious culture of binge drinking which is leading to anti-social behaviour, violence, crime and health issues. The government recognises the growing problem and seeks to tackle it by introducing new minimum pricing laws, laws restricting alcohol availability, laws restricting alcohol advertising, and laws restricting distribution.

- Society is developing an obesity problem that is fast approaching critical levels and putting a strain on the economy. To tackle the problem, the government decides to introduce laws restricting fast food advertising, laws on minimum fast food nutritional requirements, laws banning fast food outlets within a certain radius of schools, laws on food labelling and laws that increase taxes on unhealthy food.

- Society is under threat from terrorists who are plotting death and destruction. To tackle the problem, the government introduces new laws that allow phone monitoring and email interception, even of ordinary citizens. They also introduce laws allowing CCTV cameras to monitor our movements. They introduce laws on ID cards, laws that allow detention in prison without charge and laws that allow private data to be accessed by government officials.

- People use their freedom of speech to incite acts of terror against innocent civilians. The government responds by introducing 'hate speech' laws that take away the right to freely express opinions. True freedom of speech quickly vanishes.

- The banks act recklessly by using their freedom to pursue greed and self-interest. As a result they put the global economy in jeopardy. Governments tackle the problem by introducing new laws, regulations and taxes to monitor, curb and restrict the operations of the banks.

- Newspaper journalists are found to be using their freedom to act immorally and have been hacking private phone messages to get stories. The government tackles the problem by imposing new laws and regulations that curb, monitor and restrict the freedom of the press.

- A mother loses her daughter in a car accident because a driver was drunk. Even though there are existing drink driving laws, the mother campaigns tirelessly to get new, tighter laws, harsher laws introduced so that it can never happen again.

Similarly, a father loses his son after he is hit by a train at a level crossing. The father campaigns tirelessly to get new laws and regulations imposed upon the rail companies and harsher penalties for negligence so that it never happens again.

What is happening in all these scenarios is basically this: the people are using their freedom to be reckless, greedy, self-serving, indulgent, hedonistic, sinful and licentious, and then the government is trying to cure the problem with legalism.

What they're basically saying each time is, *"because you are using your freedom to do evil, we're going to have to legislate to take some of that freedom away. If you won't behave properly, we'll have to make you behave properly by force of law."*

They're doing exactly what the Pharisees did.

It's the man-made solution for sinful behaviour. More laws. Stricter laws. Harsher laws.

As our study has already revealed, not only is this method of tackling sin completely futile because law has no power to change hearts and indeed, just gives unregenerate hearts more laws to break, but by piling mountains of laws on top of the citizens, we are becoming ever more restricted, controlled, suffocated, crushed and oppressed by our governments. Liberty is slowly evaporating and we citizens are becoming less and less free.

In fact, we are not free.

We tend to think that by virtue of our citizenship in a Western democracy that we are. But if you want to put it to the test, I invite you to preach the truth of the Word of God in public... then wait to see how long it is before you are arrested.

It won't be long.

Freedom of thought and speech is simply a nice idea that now belongs to bygone era. And since freedom of thought and speech is the litmus test for true liberty, we are no longer free. A man who is not free to think and speak as he wishes is not free at all.

Today you are only free to express views publicly which are in-keeping with the government's. In the absence of God, governments make themselves the moral arbiters of the day and you speak your mind under the threat of prosecution from them. The term *Political Correctness* is merely a euphemism for linguistic fascism.

So you see the mechanism at work here. We're enslaved to sin in our hearts, that works itself out in our licentious behaviour and then the government tackles the problem by taking our freedoms away, leaving us oppressed.

THE RUIN OF SEXUAL LICENCE- A CASE STUDY

Let's examine this mechanism in a bit more detail by doing a case study on sexual sin.

As we've increasingly banished God from society, our moral compasses have broken and we're now sleeping around outside of marriage a lot more than previous generations. And of course, disease and pain and death has followed.

Sexually transmitted infections are rising. In England between 1998 and 2009, they rose by 74%. Similar rises are visible in most Western countries.

According to findings by the Jubilee Centre, the direct cost of this sexual immorality to the British National Health Service (NHS), funded by the tax payer, is more than £1 billion per year. Sexual promiscuity has also led to more unwanted pregnancies which costs the NHS £63million per year. Much of this cost comes from abortion procedures. Overall, 96% of abortions are paid for by the NHS at a cost of £118 million per year.

Going beyond the initial impact of disease and abortion, which is just murder of unborn children, sexual immorality causes psychological and emotional damage to those involved, breeds distrust, jealousy and contributes towards the breakdown of relationships and family units. As we learned in the first chapter, wounded people wound people and the cancer of hurt and pain spreads through society.

If babies born outside of marriage are not aborted they are increasingly raised in single parent families, normally by the mothers, without fathers. The cost of such family breakdown to the tax payer in the UK is estimated to be £42billion which represents 6% of public spending for 2011. It equates to £1400 for every tax payer in the UK, which is one third of the entire health budget, or about the same as the defence budget or the interest on the national debt.

In other words, Britain could wipe out the interest on its national debt if we wiped out sexual promiscuity.

Most of the financial cost to the country comes from the payment of tax credits, single parent benefits and in dealing with the health, crime and educational impact - statistics clearly show that people who grow up in single gender homes are more likely to commit crime, go to jail, themselves perpetuate the problem by having children outside of wedlock, have problems with sexual identity, drop out of school, abuse drugs, join gangs, have relational issues, experience emotional trouble, commit suicide and live in poverty. All of these things then have knock-on effects on their children and their children and upon society as a whole. The consequences of sin ripple through society making the whole thing worse than it was before, emotionally, mentally, physically and financially.

As people then feel the world around them get colder and more selfish, they experience more pain and become harder too, putting up barriers and becoming ever more cynical and pessimistic. Sin begets sin and the downward spiral of moral entropy gathers pace. Eventually, moral collapse left unchecked will bring the entire society to complete social and economic ruin.

If we tally up the economic cost of sexual licence in the UK, taking into account the knock on effect that ripples throughout society, the figure is estimated by the Jubilee Centre to begin at around £100 billion per year. £100 billion is about twice the total cost to the economy of alcohol abuse, smoking and obesity combined and represents one ninth of the total UK national debt. In other words, if these estimates from the Jubilee Centre are correct and notwithstanding interest rate fluctuations, by wiping out sexual promiscuity alone, we could pay off all national debt within a decade.

After that decade of debt repayment had passed, we would then have £100 billion per year to invest in schools, hospitals, city beautification, lower taxes, parks, infrastructure and anything else that was required.

And remember this is just one sin.

Very simply, our immorality is spreading chaos, fear and disease and is bankrupting us in the process. So even the state of the economy rests entirely on heart regeneration. Societal moral collapse leads to financial collapse. Society cannot survive without God.

"Surrender to all our desires obviously leads to impotence, disease, jealousies, lies, concealment, and everything that is the reverse of health, good humour, and frankness. For any happiness, even in this world, quite a lot of restraint is going to be necessary." - CS Lewis

The Bible has shown two ways to tackle licentiousness - the Pharisaic, man-made, legalistic way which tries to use external coercion to restrain from without...and which doesn't work...and which leads to oppression...or the Spirit-filled way of Jesus, which transforms people from within and which leads to genuine freedom.

A government of godly men and women would recognise the heart problem and would help make Jesus Christ the centre of our lives. Unfortunately we don't have a government of godly men and women and so their only remaining option is the Pharisaic route - the imposition of ever stricter laws. It's when the laws really start becoming oppressive that you know your society is crumbling.

The Roman historian Tacitus rightly said, *"The more corrupt the state, the more numerous the laws."*

GETTING AROUND THE LAWS

Initially when the citizens feel the pressure of unjust laws they just try to find ways around them. The laws don't change their desires so they keep on doing whatever it is they want to do. When America brought in prohibition, the citizens just got creative with alcohol consumption went underground. They found a way to beat the system.

In the 18th Century, the governments of England, Scotland and France decided that they were going to introduce a window tax law. Under this law, people had to pay tax based on the number of windows they had in their house. Did the people pay the tax? No, they just found a way around the law. They simply bricked up some of their windows to avoid paying the tax. So widespread was this method of beating the system that the citizens started developing health problems from the lack of sunlight reaching them in their windowless houses. The law didn't make people behave in the right way and it didn't change their hearts. It just created new problems that needed new laws, because unregenerate people just found a way around them.

In the Netherlands a tax was introduced on the width of the buildings. Did the people then simply pay more tax? Of course not. They simply built their houses extra narrow and tall so that they would have the same amount of space without having to pay excessive tax. Again, the government created laws to control and restrict and the people found ways around them.

As people find new ways of getting round those laws, other laws are needed to close the loopholes, and then more laws are needed to define those loopholes and so on and so on. Just like what we saw with the Pharisees.

Before long, people are buried under a mound of oppressive, crushing laws and no one has really changed. In the meantime, in the same way that children get resentful and rebellious when they grow up under religious legalism, the citizens get resentful and rebellious when they grow up under governmental legalism. People start to despise the system.

This is dangerous for the government and for the structure of society because ultimately, when the government has thrown enough laws at the people, and when the people begin to feel suffocated and oppressed, and when they feel like they have no freedom anymore, and when they see the hypocrisy and corruption of their leaders, and when they see the state becoming the measure of all things, and when they find themselves in bondage and ruin, and when the tyranny reaches a crescendo, there comes a time when the people snap, and revolution soon follows.

There comes a time when people decide it would be better to die fighting for freedom against their oppressors that to continue living under the regime.

Thomas Jefferson saw this so clearly that he believed it was part of a necessary cycle. He said, *"the tree of liberty must be refreshed from time to time by the blood of patriots and tyrants."*

Such a cycle reminds us of Alexander Tytler's theory too:

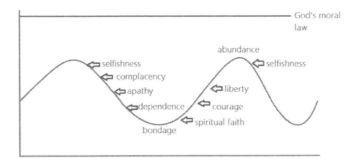

Our licentious living will lead the government to create laws that will put us into bondage and then when things get too oppressive, there will follow an uprising.

CS Lewis saw this cycle as well. He wrote:

"What Satan put into the heads of our remote ancestors was the idea that they could 'be like gods'—could set up on their own as if they had created themselves—be their own masters—invent some sort of happiness for themselves outside God, apart from God. And out of that hopeless attempt has come nearly all that we call human history—money, poverty, ambition, war, prostitution, classes, empires, slavery—the long terrible story of man trying to find something other than God which will make him happy.

The reason why it can never succeed is this. God made us: invented us as a man invents an engine. A car is made to run on gasoline, and it would not run properly on anything else. Now God designed the human machine to run on Himself. He Himself is the fuel our spirits were designed to burn, or the food our spirits were designed to feed on. There is no other. That is why it is just no good asking God to make us happy in our own way without bothering about religion. God cannot give us a happiness and peace apart from Himself, because it is not there. There is no such thing.

That is the key to history. Terrific energy is expended—civilizations are built up—excellent institutions devised; but each time something goes wrong. Some fatal flaw always brings the selfish and cruel people to the top and it all slides back into misery and ruin. In fact, the machine conks. It seems to start up all right and runs a few yards, and then it breaks down. They are trying to run it on the wrong juice. That is what Satan has done to us humans." (Mere Christianity)

The sinful human heart leads us to ruin, the governments try to control it with legalism, they become corrupt with the power in the process, the society deteriorates, hearts become colder and harder, hypocrisy increases, entropy takes hold, the whole thing falls into bondage.

"If we are not governed by God then we will be ruled by tyrants." - William Penn

PAXMAN V BORIS

Here's a real life transcript of an interview between BBC journalist, *Jeremy Paxman* and Mayor of London, *Boris Johnson*. To set the scene for this transcript, it's a few years after the economic collapse of 2008/09 and the people on the streets of London are starting to voice their resentment that the super-rich bankers who caused the problem are going about their lives unaffected, while the average person on the street is still struggling to get by.

Jeremy Paxman (Interviewer): *People are increasingly conscious of the number of people, whether they be Russian oligarchs, fleeing African despots, Arabian sheikhs, or anyone else who are walking the streets of this city [London], and against whom, frankly, they begin to feel rather resentful.*

Boris Johnson (Mayor of London): *You're talking about the sort of resentment of the super-rich?*

JP: *Yes.*

BJ: *I understand people feel alienated and they feel very hostile and suspicious. What I want to do...I don't want to harm the wealth generating, the tax generating potential of this city but I do want to see these people that you describe showing much more commitment.*

JP: *What do they do for us?*

BJ: *Well, I think what they could do is give a lot more. This city is built very largely on the generosity and philanthropy of dynamic people in the 19th Century who made colossal sums of money and who then built schools and founded hospitals and orphanages and what makes me...*

JP: *They're not doing it now...*

BJ: *They're not doing it now!*

JP: *And they should!*

BJ: *They should do it now. And it's quite incredible to me that people can walk away with multi- million pound bonuses and not understand that what people want see is them doing what the great titans did in the Victorian era.*

JP: *If they refuse to do it, is it not the obligation of the state to take sufficient money from them by force of law to ensure that it is done?*

BJ: *That is the obvious answer.*

JP: *Yes.*

BJ: *The trouble with that answer is that you end up with a tax burden that is frankly a deterrent to investment and to enterprise in London. So you're right to put it that way but that is the dilemma.*

JP: *Why did the morality of capitalism change in that way? What happened to benevolent capitalism?*

BJ: *<shakes his head and looks out the window at the city of London> I think people got into a kind of mindset which I think is quite wrong...because tax advanced and people felt they were paying more and more of their income in taxation they somehow thought they'd made their contribution. They somehow started to think their obligations were over. And they fail to see that a huge gap is opening up between the super-rich and the rest of society frankly. And I think they need to understand that.*

JP: *That gap's potentially really dangerous isn't it?*

BJ: *It's not healthy. There are huge numbers of people in this city who are making an awful lot of money. We want them here, we want them to make money, we want them to generate jobs and growth for the rest of society. But they've got to understand that they're lucky to be here - it's a fantastic city to live in - and they could make a much, much bigger contribution.*

So here's what basically happened in that exchange. Jeremy Paxman says that there are all these super rich people serving only themselves with their money and that it's a problem. They're not using their freedom well. The Mayor agrees but remembers that there was once a time in the 19th Century when rich people didn't serve themselves but instead used their freedom and their riches to benefit others. They freely donated their money to build schools, hospitals, orphanages and generally improved society with their generosity and charity.

But they're not doing it now and both agree on that point. Then we see Paxman falling into the trap of suggesting that if they no longer do it by their own free will they should be forced to do it by law i.e. taxes. If they won't hand over the money freely the government should just take the money from them, right?*

At this point the Mayor says if that they did that then all the rich people would just find a way around the laws by leaving the city and conducting their business from elsewhere. And that would be to the detriment of the city of London and the UK economy. You can't make men good by law. They just find loopholes and ways around the laws.

They then both scratch their heads at this conundrum and wonder aloud why the morality and benevolence of the city-folk has taken such a nose-dive. Why are they so selfish now? Where's the charity and generosity gone? Why are they using their free-will to serve only themselves?

Boris shakes his head and stares out the window look for an answer. They just can't understand it. What has happened to people's benevolence? What went wrong? People know *something* has gone wrong but they can't see what.

The Mayor then finishes by saying that when the law is already very severe it builds a resentment in the population that the government is taking so much of their money and they start to adopt a begrudging 'minimum requirement' mentality. Jeremy hints that the resentment is dangerous and may eventually lead to rebellion.

See the pattern?

The people using their freedom licentiously, authorities try to tackle it with legalism, people initially try to find ways around the laws to beat the system and ultimately, if oppressed enough, it leads to rebellion.

CHRIST IS THE ANSWER FOR SOCIETY

As we already know, Christ is the answer. The Spirit which cures our heart sickness is the answer. Everything else we try will fail. You can't make men good by law and without good men you can't have a good society. So you must go on to think of how to make good men who *know* the MORAL LAW and who *choose* the MORAL LAW.

If you do that, you not only keep society good, but you keep it *free*.

Edmund Burke said, *"Men qualify for freedom in exact proportion to their disposition to put moral chains on their own appetites. Society cannot exist unless a controlling power is put somewhere on the will and appetite, and the less of it there is within, the more there must be without. It is ordained in the eternal constitution of things that men of intemperate minds cannot be free. Their passions forge their fetters."*

Spanish philosopher, statesman and writer, Juan Donoso-Cortes said, *"There are only two possible forms of control: one internal and the other external; religious control and political control. They are of such a nature that when the [internal] religious barometer rises, the barometer of [external] falls and likewise, when the [internal] religious barometer falls, the [external] political barometer, that is political control and tyranny rises. That is the law humanity, a law of history. If civilised man falls into disbelief and immorality, the way is prepared for some gigantic and colossal tyrant, universal and immense."*

Either God, by his Holy Spirit rules within our hearts or secular powers will try enslave from without. Burke went on to say, *"True religion is the foundation of society. When that is once shaken by contempt the whole fabric cannot be stable or lasting."*

Benjamin Rush rightly said, *"Without Virtue there can be no liberty."* Where does virtue come from? Who is the Good Apple by which we understand bad apples? Who is the Absolute Light by which we understand darkness? Exactly. Without God there can be no liberty.

"Will power does not change men. Time does not change men. Christ does." - Henry Drummond

Even people with no Christian leanings can see this truth. The following is a quotation from Top Gear's James May, in an interview he did for the Mail on Sunday's magazine.

"A surgeon once told me, surgery is a sign of failure because it's a last resort. Which I think is a very healthy view. I think we should be trying to encourage society to heal itself, and I don't think you do that with rules. There's an ever increasing burden of paperwork and administration and computer passwords and tax codes already on people's shoulders and I'm not sure how much more we can bear. We're going to be like Rome, completely submerged in bureaucracy and unable to do anything else because there won't be the time or the energy. So I think, yes, fewer rules is something to aim for...My personal views...are that I like the idea of a society that tries to reduce rules, reduces interference and encourages individual open

mindedness and freedom of thought. That's how I feel." – James May (Live 25 Sep 2011)

*NB: I have often heard it said that the Bible is a socialistic book but this is not true. There is a big difference between charitable giving from love which the Bible prescribes and the legalistic taking and redistribution of wealth by force of government, as prescribed by socialism.

CHAPTER 19
IN SUMMARY

Without Christ we can never be internally free. And if we are not internally free, we cannot long be physically, socially or socially free. Once we begin to collapse internally, we begin to collapse as a society. Again, society cannot last unless the majority of men do the right thing when no one is watching. And that takes internal renovation. Anything else is futile.

If we don't experience this heart renovation, we will bounce back and forth endlessly between the two pits of legalism and licence and our extra dislike of one will force us into the other. Both pits lead to oppression, disease, despair and death.

We *need* Jesus Christ to stay free.

In summary:

- Christ frees us from our own sinful nature.
- Christ frees us from moral entropy.
- Christ frees us from the Law of Moses.
- Christ frees us from the death the law brings.
- Christ frees us from religious legalism.
- Christ frees us from governmental oppression.
- Christ frees us from societal collapse.

"So Christ has truly set us free. Now make sure that you stay free, and don't get tied up again in slavery to the law." (Galatians 5:1)

CHAPTER 20
THE GREAT COMMISSION

So Christ is the answer. And as we explored earlier in this book, the church is the channel through which the world should hear about him.

Paul wrote, *"But how can they call on him to save them unless they believe in him? And how can they believe in him if they have never heard about him? And how can they hear about him unless someone tells them?" (Romans 10:14)*

And of course the answer is that they can't. We need to tell them. The church needs to mobilise itself to bring the gospel of freedom into a world that desperately needs to hear it. We need to be salt and light. A city on a hill. We need to go about it any way we can. Preach, sign petitions, campaign, start initiatives, movements, prayer groups, evangelism projects, marches...anything. Anything that gives people a chance to respond to Jesus Christ.

Jesus has commanded this of us saying, *"Therefore, go and make disciples of all the nations, baptizing them in the name of the Father and the Son and the Holy Spirit. Teach these new disciples to obey all the commands I have given you. And be sure of this: I am with you always, even to the end of the age."(Matt 28:19-20)*

That's basically what The Fuel Project is all about. It's about mobilising the church to fulfil the great commission. It's about **informing** the church so that it's equipped with a knowledge and wisdom of the Bible and can defend and spread the gospel.

It's about **inspiring** the church so that it dares to live courageously and by faith. And it's about **igniting** real evangelism activities in real communities so that people actually get to see and hear about the love of Christ and get a chance to respond to it themselves.

CIVIL DISOBEDIENCE

Now because of how far society has slipped, Christians are unfortunately seen as the enemy. People have lost sight of the meaning of good and evil and so, we're seen as the bad guys. Christian viewpoints are no longer tolerated in many places and persecution is growing. Any Christian that challenges the prevailing darkness is going to experience some level of persecution.

There have been a myriad of reports recently that confirm this. Christian cafe owners being threatened with arrest for displaying Bible verses on their TV screens. Christian foster carers being banned from adopting children because of their views on homosexuality. Christians being banned from wearing crosses around their neck at work and some losing their jobs for refusing to go against their conscience. The government making it illegal for pastors to refuse to marry gay people in church. Speaking God's word in public becoming illegal under new 'hate speech' laws. Christian midwives being told they can no longer opt out of assisting with abortions. The government interfering in Christian parenting, threatening to remove children from parents who insist on the exclusivity of Jesus. The freedom to remove children from sex education classes, which promotes homosexuality, coming under attack.

In fact the civil law is starting to contradict God's MORAL LAW in almost every sphere of life and Christians are under increasing pressure to abandon their principles and to conform to the ideology of the age. We can't do that. And that may mean civil disobedience.

I only say this to warn of the kind of atmosphere we're going into so that no one will be caught out. Remember when Jesus was sending out his disciples he said, *"Go! I am sending you out like sheep among wolves." (Luke 10:3)*

We're going to be like sheep among wolves...but we must still go. And we must follow the Spirit at all times, even if that means contradicting immoral laws.

Albert Einstein said of civil disobedience, *"Never do anything against conscience, even if the state demands it."*

And that's pretty much the message of the Bible too.

The Bible tells us that we should follow the civil law at all times *until* such a point that it contradicts the MORAL LAW but that when the two diverge, we must go with the MORAL LAW.

Now let us tread carefully here lest we be accused of sedition, and firstly emphasise how important it is that Christians follow the civil law to the best of their ability.

Paul tells us, *"Everyone must submit to governing authorities. For all authority comes from God, and those in positions of authority have been placed there by God. So anyone who rebels against authority is rebelling against what God has instituted, and they will be punished. For the authorities do not strike fear in people who are doing right, but in those who are doing wrong. Would you like to live without fear of the authorities? Do what is right, and they will honour you. The authorities are God's servants, sent for your good. But if you are doing wrong, of course you should be afraid, for they have the power to punish you. They are God's servants, sent for the very purpose of punishing those who do what is wrong. So you must submit to them, not only to avoid punishment, but also to keep a clear conscience. Pay your taxes, too, for these same reasons. For government workers need to be paid. They are serving God in what they do. Give to everyone what you owe them: Pay your taxes and government fees to those who collect them, and give respect and honour to those who are in authority."(Rom 13:1-8)*

So Paul is urging the Christians in Rome to be model citizens. In fact, he urges us to pray for those in authority saying:

"I urge you, first of all, to pray for all people. Ask God to help them; intercede on their behalf and give thanks for them. Pray this way for kings and all who are in authority so that we can live peaceful and quiet lives marked by godliness and dignity." (1 Tim 2:1-2)

Titus tells us, *"Remind the believers to submit to the government and its officers. They should be obedient, always ready to do what is good." (Titus 3:1)*

Peter tells us, *"For the Lord's sake respect all human authority - whether the king as head of state, or the officials he has appointed...don't use your freedom as an excuse to do evil...Respect everyone and love your Christian brothers and sisters. Fear God, and respect the king."* (1 Pet 2:13-14, 16-17)

And of course, Jesus himself, when asked about whether to pay taxes said, *"Give to Caesar what belongs to Caesar."* (Luke 20:25)

The Bible is clear that Christians are called to be the best citizens in society.

However, when the civil laws bring us into conflict with God's eternal MORAL LAW and his commands, we must part ways and follow God only.

Daniel is a great example of this. The officials in Babylon were looking for a trumped up crime that they could charge him for but when they tried to dig up some dirt to convict him, they actually couldn't find any:

"He was always faithful, always responsible, and completely trustworthy." (Dan 6:4)

He was a model citizen.

So to trap him they decided to create a law that they knew he wouldn't keep. They passed a law that contradicted God's MORAL LAW saying that anyone who prayed to anyone other than the king should be executed. Of course Daniel couldn't do this because he would then be guilty of idolatry - only God should receive our prayers. So when he learned about the new law he simply *"went home and knelt down as usual in his upstairs room with its window open towards Jerusalem. He prayed three times a day just as he always had done, giving thanks to God."* (Dan 6:10) Daniel was thrown into the lion's den for this crime but God famously honoured him for his courage and integrity by shutting the mouths of the lions, and he was not killed.

A similar thing happened with Shadrach, Meschach and Abednego. They were ordered by King Nebuchadnezzar to bow down and worship an idol. Rather than go against God they refused to obey the orders and when they did Nebuchadnezzar was so furious that he threatened to throw them into a fiery furnace. The three Godly boys responded boldly saying, *"O Nebuchadnezzar, we do not need to defend ourselves before you. If we are thrown into the blazing furnace, the God whom we serve is able to save us. He will rescue us from your power, your Majesty. But even if he doesn't, we want to make it clear to you, Your Majesty, that we will never serve your gods or worship the golden statue you have set up."* (Dan 3:18) They too were saved from their executions by God.

We find the same courage and integrity in the apostles who were dragged in front of city officials and told to stop spreading the gospel of Jesus. They defiantly replied, *"We must obey God rather than any human authority"* (Acts 5:29). The Bible reports that they then *"continued to teach and preach this message: 'Jesus is the Messiah.'"* They too consequently found themselves in and out of jail, facing beatings in the process. They actually became proud of their scars because they knew for Whom they suffered and it gave them a chance to identify with the suffering of their Saviour.

Indeed, throughout all history, this has always been the way of things for Christians. To be the most peaceful, law abiding, trust-worthy and faithful citizens in a community up until such point where the government turns on them and tells them to contradict their conscience and the MORAL LAW. At this point they diverge from the civil law and continue following God regardless of the consequences. They have done this, and we must also do this.

Early Christians in Rome were persecuted for not bowing down to Caesar or worshipping pagan gods. The Reformers and Bible translators were pursued, jailed and killed for giving the Bible to people in their own languages. John Bunyan protested about freedom of religion and was frequently imprisoned. The abolitionists and people like Martin Luther King Jr. employed civil disobedience for their cause. People like Dietrich Bonhoeffer and Martin Niemoller resisted the Nazis. These and many others like them faced prison and death, preferring to be faithful to God rather than accept immoral laws. And that's our responsibility also. Martin Luther King, Jr. said, *"We must never forget that everything Adolf Hitler did in Germany was 'legal' and everything the Hungarian freedom fighters did in Hungary was 'illegal'"* What's legal and illegal comes second to what's moral and immoral. Where God and man contradict one another, we must follow God.

Alexander Bickel said, *"We cannot, by total reliance on law, escape the duty to judge right and wrong...There are good laws and there are occasionally bad laws, and it conforms to the highest traditions of a free society to offer resistance to bad laws, and to disobey them."*

Clarence Darrow said, *"As long as the world shall last there will be wrongs, and if no man objected and no man rebelled, those wrongs would last forever."*

Martin Luther King Jr. again said, *"Never, never be afraid to do what's right, especially if the well-being of a person or animal is at stake. Society's punishments are small compared to the wounds we inflict on our soul when we look the other way."*

Jesus himself said, *"Don't be afraid of those who want to kill your body; they cannot touch your soul. Fear only God, who can destroy both soul and body in hell."* - Matthew 10:28

All of these quotations inform us of the principle that God is our highest moral authority. He is the Good Apple and the Midday Sun by which we make all our moral judgements. These words of wisdom further inform us that government, when it decides to detach itself from God, is actually capable of great evil and oppression and that such things should be opposed for the good of all.

They further tell us that submission to government does not mean uncritical obedience - we don't become machines who can shirk responsibility for our actions. When the Nazi officials told the soldiers to gas innocent humans in concentration camps, the individual soldiers still had a decision to make about whether to obey. Immoral laws contrary to God's will are to be disobeyed.

Now Christian civil disobedience should always be non-violent and those who engage in it should be willing to face the consequences. But as Luther King Jr. says, the wounds society inflicts are small compared to the wounds we inflict on our soul when we go along with immoral laws. Don't be manipulated or intimidated into silence. The world needs our courage.

And finally we must not think of persecution for being a Christian as something unusual. To those of us who come from Western countries with a Christian influence, it may seem unusual to us, but the truth is that we have been the exceptions to the rule. Throughout all history, and even in most parts of the world today, suffering has been, and remains, the norm for Christians. Jesus told His disciples, *"This is my command: Love each other. "If the world hates you, remember that it hated me first. The world would love you as one of its own if you belonged to it, but you are no longer part of the world. I chose you to* come out of the world, so it hates you. Do you remember what I told you? 'A slave is not greater than the master.' Since they persecuted me, naturally they will persecute you. And if they had listened to me, they would listen to you. They will do all this to you because of me, for they have rejected the One who sent me. They would not be guilty if I had not come and spoken to them. But now they have no excuse for their sin. Anyone who hates me also hates my Father." (John 15:17-23)

He prayed for us saying, "The world hates them because they do not belong to the world, just as I do not belong to the world. I'm not asking you to take them out of the world, but to keep them safe from the evil one. They do not belong to this world any more than I do. Make them holy by your truth; teach them your word, which is truth. Just as you sent me into the world, I am sending them into the world. And I give myself as a holy sacrifice for them so they can be made holy by your truth." (John 17:14-19)

We will be hated. We have to get used to that. It's a natural consequence of belonging to Jesus in a world ruled by the evil one. We have to try to love and save those who would persecute us anyway.

Finally, it was Peter who wrote, "be happy when you are insulted for being a Christian, for then the glorious Spirit of God rests upon you. If you suffer, however, it must not be for murder, stealing, making trouble, or prying into other people's affairs. But it is no shame to suffer for being a Christian. Praise God for the privilege of being called by his name!" (1 Peter 4:12-16)

If we're to suffer, it can't be for immoral behaviour.

We can't defend the MORAL LAW by breaking the MORAL LAW. We must in all other senses be perfect citizens. But it is no shame to be persecuted for being a Christian who obeys the will of God.

Chapter 21
The Fuel Vision

Right then, it's time to get our hands dirty.

The vision for the Fuel Project is to mobilise the church to go out into the world courageously challenging corruption, injustice, immorality and Godlessness and spreading the uncompromising gospel about an uncompromising Saviour to the four corners of the world.

How are we going to do that?

The Wilberforce Method

One of the most inspirational people of all time for me was William Wilberforce. William Wilberforce was an English politician who lived in the late 1700's and early 1800's and he became a Christian as a young man. Initially he thought that his conversion to Christianity should perhaps mean retirement from public life altogether and a life of solitude. However, after a little thought and persuasion from his friends, he rightly decided that the principles of Christianity should lead not just to isolated meditation and prayer, but also to action, and from that point onwards he spent his life using his position and resources to achieve two main goals; goals that he felt that God himself had set before him.

The first goal, for which he is most famous, was the abolition of the slave trade. The second goal was the reformation of society.

Wilberforce's society looked a lot like ours - it was on a downward moral curve. It was the post-Enlightenment period where Christianity was stigmatised and people who adhered too enthusiastically to their faith were seen as irrational fanatics. It wasn't considered polite to bring Jesus up in conversation and even those who went to church were nominal Anglicans at best.

As might be expected, with God being shunned from public life, the general welfare of society was disintegrating. Immorality was running rampant around the country, brothels had become acceptable and indeed, quite fashionable, and it had started to lead towards paedophilia with girls of 12 and 13 being dragged into the system. Drunkenness was out of control and this had led to violence and riots. Criminals carried out their deeds shamelessly in broad daylight and an analysis in 1796 concluded that the people of London engaged in a shocking catalogue of human depravity. In fact, it was estimated that about an eighth of all citizens in London at the time were supporting themselves through illegal activity, from prostitution to thieving to embezzlement to fraud.

As I said, it looked a lot like today.

It had shunned its moral compass and the entropy of sin was turning the whole thing into chaos. Wilberforce rightly believed that the only way to improve society was to give God back His place. He said:

"To the decline of Religion and Morality our national difficulties must both directly and indirectly be chiefly ascribed; and my only solid hopes for the well-being of my country depend, not so much on her fleets and armies, not so much on the wisdom of her rulers, or the spirit of her people, as on the persuasion that she still contains many, who love and obey the Gospel of Christ;

that their intercessions may yet prevail; that for the sake of these, Heaven may still look upon us with an eye of favour." William Wilberforce (p272)

He also said: *"If a principle of true religion should...gain ground, there is no estimating the effects on public morals, and the consequent influence on our political welfare."* – William Wilberforce (p276)

Again he said: *"It is only by educating our people in Christian principles that we can advance in strength, greatness and happiness."*

In other words he recognised, as we should, that if society was to change for the better, it needed Jesus Christ. And that Christians were the channels through which people should hear about Christ, by turning their faith into action.

For Wilberforce that meant campaigning, preaching, signing petitions, lobbying, handing out tracts and pamphlets and raising public awareness in any way possible. In Amazing Grace, the movie that depicts Wilberforce's story, he says, *"We are talking about the truth, so we should hand it out to people, drop it from church rooves, paint pictures of it, write songs about...make pies out of it!"* In other words, use every gift, talent, resource, opportunity and specialist knowledge we have to get the truth out there into the public realm. What I described in *Know Your Enemy* as fighting the 'information war'.

In order to do this effectively, he set up many *societies*. These societies, in effect, were small groups or specialist platoons made up of people with complementary skills, passions and resources. They worked together to bring the gospel into various targeted areas of public life. As recorded in

Wilberforce's biography, he believed that using Christianity to reform the moral framework of the country was the ultimate issue. If carried out successfully, it would make more of a difference to daily lives and save more souls than any number of well-intentioned Acts of Parliament.

And so, he and the people around him set up The Society for the Suppression of Vice, the Church Mission Society, the Proclamation Society, The Bible Society, The Society for the Prevention of Cruelty to Animals, the Small Debt Society, the Abolition Society, the Anti-Slavery Society, the Sunday School Society, the Bettering Society and many more. Each of these societies targeted a specific social ill or were designed to spread the Gospel in some new way, and in order to raise awareness of their causes they wrote books, tracts, pamphlets, campaigned, lobbied and generally did anything necessary to get their message out. They fought the information war. They made sure the gospel was heard.

Wilberforce himself wrote a book called 'Practical Christianity' challenging Christians of the day to turn their faith into action believing all Christians should use their time to *"find some ignorance to instruct, some wrong to redress, some want to supply, some misery to alleviate."* Simply putting the Law of Christ into effect by loving God and others in practical and positive ways.

The group of people around Wilberforce that formed the engine of the movement are today known as *The Clapham Sect* but in their time they were mockingly referred to as *'The Saints'*. As usual, the world didn't particularly like this group of sanctimonious Christians who were making everyone else look bad, bothering their consciences and fighting to raise the moral standards of the day, and so they received much opposition.

Yet when I consider them, I see in them the best representation of a true Christian community that has been committed to history outside of the Book of Acts. In fact, although I call this 'the Wilberforce method' it's really 'the Acts method'. I only talk about Wilberforce to prove that the New Testament church wasn't a one-off. And that if we got our act together, we could have just a big an impact for God's kingdom.

Historian Stephen Tomkins describes *The Clapham Sect* as *"a network of friends and families in England, with William Wilberforce as its centre of gravity, who were powerfully bound together by their shared moral and spiritual values, by their religious mission and social activism, by their love for each other, and by marriage."*

William Hague, in his biography of Wilberforce, describes how *The Saints* lived within close proximity to one another and how they would be constantly engaged in strategic planning and practical application of the word of God. He says, *"The Saints were an informal community, characterised by considerable intimacy as well as commitment to practical Christianity and an opposition to slavery. They developed a relaxed family atmosphere, wandering freely in and out of each other's homes and gardens, and discussing the many religious, social and political topics that engaged them."*

We see that same kind of familial, informal atmosphere where believers meet every day, sharing their lives together, in the Biblical descriptions of the early church. I believe it's what true Christian community looks like. What they effectively created was a church that didn't just meet and pray together but which put faith into action together. They had a mission and they worked at it.

Because of their tireless efforts, they did indeed change the country, and by consequence, the world beyond. Tomkins says, *"the ethos of Clapham became the spirit of the age."* Indeed, it is reckoned that, along with the great preachers of the day, they were primarily responsible for the raised spiritual climate which would echo right down into the Victorian era. That same era that Boris Johnson, Mayor of London, pointed to wistfully, for examples of prosperous titans who used their wealth for the benefit of others. That period from Wilberforce's time to the end of the Victorian era is also noted for its vast social and economic improvements in Britain. The country became healthier, more prosperous and militarily powerful during that time. In fact, it became so powerful that it rose to develop the largest geographical empire in world history.

And it's as simple as that. These 'Saints', who were mocked in their time, primarily reformed the morals of society by putting God back in the hearts of the men and women who had forgotten him and left the world a better place for it. This is the potential of a small group of Christians who are just willing to put faith into action and spread the Gospel of Jesus Christ. Margaret Mead famously said, *"Never doubt that a small group of thoughtful, committed citizens can change the world. Indeed, it is the only thing that ever has."* She's right. Just ask the 12 disciples.

The reason that I personally find Wilberforce and the Saints so inspirational is because the method they employed to reach the world was my vision for the Fuel Project long before I had ever heard of them.

The goal is to have a network of people coming together in small group communities all over the world - each person within the group having their own God given gift, passion and set of skills. These groups will be relaxed, informal, family type structures. They will be bound by their love for one another and their shared goals for spreading the gospel and making an impact in their communities.

Because of modern technology, we can now do this on a worldwide scale, sharing teaching and training materials, ideas, and we can use the internet to help people find one another for fellowship. To that end, we have set up a "Directory Map" at thefuelproject.org. Hundreds of people are adding themselves to the directory so that other believers can find them for fellowship. Small groups are developing all around the world.

For more information on how and why the church needs to go about reaching our communities, please read or watch *The Restless Church*. The Restless Church is the sequel to this book. It details why the church is currently so ineffective in reaching our culture and why a return to the Acts Method (the Wilberforce Method) is needed.

With the small groups coming together, the aim of the Fuel Project is to produce more materials that will inform, inspire and ignite the church into action. This will primarily be done through a series of videos called "Kindling". These 30-60 minute videos will be designed for use by the small groups and will contain a mixture of teaching, group discussion questions, and practical demonstrations to follow.

If you have a group that would like to help inspire the church to action by being a part of the Kindling video series, please email authenticfuel@gmail.com.

If you want to find believers in your area for fellowship, you can add yourself to the Directory Map by emailing authenticfuel@gmail.com

You can also support the vision of The Fuel Project financially by making a donation by PayPal to authenticfuel@gmail.com.

"The most critical need of the Church at this moment is men, bold men, free men. The church must seek, in prayer and much humility, the coming again of men made of the stuff of which prophets and martyrs are made."- A.W. Tozer

For more information about the Fuel Project, or to get involved, please visit:

thefuelproject.org
youtube.com/thefuelproject
facebook.com/thefuelproject
twitter.com/thefuelproject
google.com/+thefuelproject

APPENDIX 1 - The Law of Christ In Action

If you'd like to make an impact in your community with your church, small group, or even individually, but need ideas, here is a list to start you off. It's a good idea to accompany all of your efforts with some kind of explanation of the gospel, whether it be by speech or by tract, but just getting into the habit of putting the Law of Christ into action i.e. loving God and others will be beneficial in the long-run.

1. Have a day doing neighbours chores for them. Knock on their doors, ask if they need their grass cut, car washed or anything from the store, then do it for them for free. Leave them with a tract or share the gospel with them before you go.

2. Invite non-Christian friends or neighbours over for dinner.

3. If you're doing anything fun with your group, invite any non-Christian friends to join and be a part of it. Let them see what Christian community is all about.

4. Skip a meal (individually or collectively) and give the money you would have spent to charity.

5. Pay someone a compliment.

6. Have a clear out and take things you don't need to a charity shop.

7. Give up your place in a queue (line) to someone else.

8. Hold a fund-raiser for a good cause.
9. Arrange a neighbourhood clean-up. Maybe wear t-shirts so people can see who you are. Be prepared to chat and share the gospel with anyone who passes.

10. Leave tracts in places where they might be found.

11. Bake things and give them away free to the community. Use any opportunities to share the gospel.

12. Buy a coffee or some food and give it to someone on the way to work.

13. At the end of the day think of three things to thank God for before you go to sleep.

14. Switch off the TV one evening and do something with your family instead. Or play games with your group.

15. Use a buy one, get one free coupon and give the free one away.

16. When you're out with friends turn off your phone, don't check Facebook or email and give them your attention.

17. Take the time to savour and thank God for good things that you normally take for granted, such as some scenery, a meal, some music, the fresh air, the sunshine, your health etc.

18. Go for a walk in your neighbourhood with your group and pray about what you see.

19. Buy something from a charity shop and pay more than what was on the price tag.

20. Give a home-made gift to a loved one.

21. Offer to babysit for friends.

22. Give blood.

23. Plant some seeds where the flowers will be seen and enjoyed by others.

24. Buy something in season from a local store rather than a supermarket.

25. Pray for someone who is unwell or in need.

26. Email or write to your local MP or local government representative regarding an issue of injustice or immorality.

27. Contact someone you haven't spoken to in a while.

28. Feed the birds.

Remember, whatever you do, be authentic, spontaneous and extravagant!

Made in the USA
Lexington, KY
05 July 2015